Published by sarahNet Ltd

Company Number 05094606

sarahNet Ltd, Shedfield, Hampshire SO32 2JE

First Published in the United Kingdom 2017

Copyright 2017 © sarahNet Ltd

ALL RIGHTS RESERVED

The moral right of the author and Illustrator has been asserted

This book is sold subject to the condition that it shall not, by way of trade or otherwise, be lent, re-sold, hired out or otherwise circulated without the publisher's prior consent in any form of binding or cover other than that in which it is published and without a similar condition including this condition being imposed on the subsequent purchaser.

ISBN-13: 978-1979611725
ISBN-10: 1979611726

Cover Illustration by Sarah Keen

# Acknowledgement

Heartfelt and most grateful thanks to the editor of this book - Sarah Keen. For the exquisite artwork and creation of the amazing front cover, I thank you once again. Such talent, understanding and depth of soul shine out through every brush stroke. A rare treasure and one I consider myself so lucky to have found.

*Lady May*

# Dedication

For Gwydion

As it is now, as it has been before and as it will be for all times.

And for my brothers.

*Lady May*

\*\*\*

# About the author

Lady May lives and works in the beautiful English county of Hampshire. She is a qualified herbalist and follows a way of life that has been passed down through her family for generations. She has taken the traditional three degrees of the Craft to become a High Priestess and Witch Queen. She is still learning.

Lady May knows she has been Blessed and greatly honoured to have been taught and mentored by some of the country's oldest, wisest Elders and followers of the Craft: Witchcraft in its truest sense as it has been practised for thousands of years, with the greatest respect for all living things.

Other works by this author:
Blessed Be – An Illustrated Walk Through A Year In The English Countryside.

# Contents

About the author ..................................................... 4

Part One : Thirteen Moons ................................. 8

Part Two – Falling Moon .................................... 42

Norfolk .................................................................. 112

And Paddy came too .......................................... 125

The day the Fith-Fath moved ........................... 130

The Seashore Ritual ............................................ 135

The Hare ............................................................... 143

# The Hare & The Sword

# Preface

Crackling embers give off a red amber glow, flames from the bonfire leap and dance high into the darkness of the night sky. Smoke rising lazily fills the air with its familiar smell and all around me people laugh and chatter, their breath billowing puffs of white vapour into the chill air.

The atmosphere is electric, full of anticipation for what the night might bring. It is October 31st, we are celebrating Samhain. More usually referred to as Halloween, it is the one night of the year when the veil between the worlds is at its thinnest. A pagan fire festival, Samhain (pronounced Sa'ween) celebrates the ending of the old year and welcomes in the new year. It is a time to say goodbye to all that we no longer want or need in our lives, a time to give thanks for all the good things that have come our way, a time to reflect upon lessons learned and make way for new beginnings, new hopes and new dreams.

And so, it is, that on this night I begin my story, a story I have waited a very long time to tell.

*Blessed Be*

# Part One : Thirteen Moons

As far back as I can remember I have lived in a very special secret world of my own, a world of knowing and understanding, a world of seeing and believing, a world that very few people even know exists. As a young girl of six or seven years of age, maybe younger, I could see and hear things that others apparently could not. I learned very early on that these experiences were best kept to myself, no one likes to be labelled a freak or a liar and I am neither. I had a very unhappy childhood and between the ages of eight and sixteen things were so awful that I often retreated into my own 'other' world, I felt safe there. I held on tightly to the fact that no matter how bad things got, there was always one person who understood me, my Grandmother, Catherine Ivy. For many years, we were forced to be apart, but she knew my Secret, she was part of it all and I longed to be with her.

For the first eight years of my life I lived with my mother, father and my two younger brothers; as far as I knew, we were a normal happy family. Dad was a boat builder and often away delivering yachts to their new owners, whilst Mum stayed at home looking after my brothers and me.

To give my mother a break from looking after three young children on her own so much I was sent to spend most weekends and school holidays with my Grandparents.

Friday afternoons during term time always seemed to drag relentlessly as I waited for the bell to ring heralding the start of the weekend. My impatience was borne from the fact that I knew Grandad Jack would be waiting for me at the school gates, his big strong arms outstretched waiting to scoop me up as I ran toward him. I loved the smell of his trench coat, it was a mixture of wax and earth, it was home. As soon as he put me back down again I would run toward his motorbike clambering eagerly into the back seat of the sidecar. There I waited listening intently for the sound of the kick-down as his foot struck the starter pedal, then came a roar from the engine and we were off and I knew Nan would be waiting.

Grandad was a gardener for the local council parks department and even when he wasn't working he spent all his time at home in his own garden. I spent hours out there with him I even had my own little veggie patch and whatever Grandad was growing, I grew some too in my own little garden. He taught me all he knew about the flora and fauna of the countryside and country ways.

Through his teachings and my own observations, I learned quickly to accept the cycles of life as being one continuous journey. I understood the concept of there being no beginning and no end, life itself was a transition from one place to another. People and animals did not just disappear when they died never to be seen again, they simply moved on somewhere else.

When I wasn't with Grandad in the garden I would be by my Nan's side copying whatever she did; watching, doing, learning. I especially loved Mondays because it was wash day. Nan and I would get out the old washing boiler, the scrub board, mangle and a pair of wooden tongs and together we set about the mornings work. One of my favourite jobs was to empty the contents of the 'blue bag' into the bath and using a great big stick I stirred it all around in the water as the sheets went in for a soaking.

I marvelled at how this dark cobalt blue powder did not stain the sheets bright blue, instead they appeared from the bath crystal white and gleaming. I watched as Nan pegged them on the line to dry, a smile appearing proudly on her face as they blew wildly in the wind.

I was never sure what the muslin 'blue bag' contained, but I vaguely remember Nan telling me it was a mixture of powders containing Gentian plant which gave the 'blue' whiteness to the linen. Blue powders that turn sheets brilliant white; it must be Magic.

Nan and I baked together, read together, played together and every afternoon at four o clock come rain or shine we went to the copse at the top of the lane. Sometimes we took a basket with us to collect berries and flowers from the hedgerow, sometimes we just enjoyed the walk, but we always, always stopped at what appeared to be an old tumble down house.

The windows were smashed, paint peeled from the woodwork, roof tiles were missing and in general the whole house was in a bad state of repair. It looked as though it had been left empty for a very long time, years probably and yet I always felt there was a strange presence about the place as if it were watching us. The doors were broken and hanging off their hinges, tattered curtains hung in shreds at the windows. As we passed by the wooden gate at the top of the pathway that led to the front door of the cottage Nan always stopped to take a bow. I remember asking her once what she was doing.

"Paying my respects", she said.

"Respects to who Nan, there's nobody there", I replied innocently.

"Just because you cannot see someone does not mean they are not there. As you grow older you will learn that often what we see is merely a mask".

I don't know why, but at that moment a chill shiver ran down my spine as we continued along our usual path. I glanced back at the cottage and as I did so, an upstairs window slammed shut causing any remaining glass to fall out and smash upon the ground below.

Nan and Grandad lived in a remote village nestled within the Hampshire countryside and were country folk through and through. Every Friday morning during school holidays, Nan and I walked the three miles to the nearest bus stop to catch the one and only bus that day that would take us to town.

Once there, we met up with Aunt Queenie, Nan's sister and together they would do their weekly shopping. I enjoyed the bus ride into the city, but for me the best part of the trip was the lunch we always had in a big department store called Edwin Jones. That and the fact that I got to choose my favourite yoghurt to take home. I can taste it now, Mandarin flavour.

Aunt Queenie and my Nan were very close and always so pleased to see each other. They spent the whole morning chattering between themselves and I often wondered how they could possibly talk so much and not be out of breath. I listened intently to their tales taking it all in, but not actually understanding what it all meant, nor did I take much notice of the times and dates that were routinely mentioned, except that they always involved either the Moon or the Sun. Perhaps they told people their horoscopes, I thought to myself.

Although I understood little of their conversation I knew it was not for everyone's ears. They often spoke quietly to each in a hushed whisper and I noticed we always sat as far away from other people as possible.

They obviously didn't want people to see the pieces of paper and little packages they passed between each other. I didn't know what was in the packages, but I guessed it probably had something to do with the fact that Nan had been busy in her kitchen the day before making all sorts of lotions, potions, creams and ointments.

I loved those afternoons, the house smelt wonderful for days afterwards. Sometimes I would help mix the ingredients together in a big china bowl and I remember to this day, the sweet smell of the herbs and the gentle ring from the bowl as the spoon struck its edges.

Aunt Queenie lived in a tiny cottage deep within the New Forest and I loved going to visit her. She kept chickens, ducks and geese and when we visited it was my job to collect the eggs. Some went on the wooden table by the gate to sell, Nan had half a dozen to take home and the rest we had for tea, boiled egg and soldiers.

Aunt Queenie's garden was huge. It was the sort of ramshackle garden that housed much of interest to a child's mind. The house had infinite places to explore and curious collections of implements. It seemed to go on for miles and miles sprawling enticingly in every direction. At the bottom of the garden there was a little wooden bridge that arched its way across a small brook leading to the open forest. It was the way we went on many an afternoon foraging from Nature's larder. We collected mushrooms, berries, nuts, fruits and blossom from the hedgerow, twigs and fir cones for the fire and all sorts of other goodies.

I especially loved spring time when I could pick bluebells, violets and wild primroses. On our return to the cottage Aunt Queenie would put the flowers I had picked in a tiny glass vase and place them with great pride in the centre of her kitchen table.

The unmistakable scent of the wild flowers soon filled the room and our hearts with joy. Violets to this day remind me of my Nan and dear Aunt Queenie and for that reason they have a very special place not only in my garden, but in my heart.

Everything we collected whilst we were foraging was discussed at great length. What it was called, why we were collecting it, if it was a food or a medicine or both. Sometimes, Nan and Aunt Queenie set me little tests, I would be sent off to find a specific plant or mushroom then I had to bring it back to them to see if I had got it right. Sometimes I got it right, sometimes I got it wrong, either way it didn't matter because all the time I was learning. I remember Nan explaining to me how important it was to know every part of every plant in the minutest of detail. She taught me that plants were like people; in our basic form, we may all look very much the same, but each one of us is an individual and totally unique in our own way. It was the little things that always made the difference.

"Nature likes to play tricks on us", she used to say, "like growing plants and flowers that look very much alike side by side and yet in their subtle differences, they are either safe or deadly. You wouldn't want to get them muddled up, now would you?" and I agreed I most certainly would not.

Little did I realise it was during these wonder-filled afternoons in the forest with Nan and Aunt Queenie that I was already being prepared for the ways of the Witch.

I remember those days with great fondness, they were happy times singing and dancing our way amongst the trees. I remember how I loved to take my shoes off and feel the bare earth beneath my feet. Soft velvety mounds of moss became a cushion for my back as I lay gazing upward through the canopy of leaves shading me from the brightness of the Sun. Sometimes we played 'Hide and Seek' and I loved to crouch down in between the gnarled roots of the Oak and the Yew trees to hide. It felt like I was being cradled by big, strong, protective arms and I felt safe there.

Often, in the stillness of waiting to be found I heard the quiet whispers of the trees as they spoke to me. It was always when I was quiet and still that these things happened. It wasn't an audible dialogue like the conversation you can hear between one person and another. I couldn't 'hear' anything out loud, I was just aware of conversations all around me.

Sometimes I listened, other times I watched as scenes began to unfold right in front of me. It was like watching a movie, I didn't speak, I didn't have to, I just watched. Then, as if a switch had been flicked, it all stopped and I carried on with whatever it was I had been doing beforehand. I was never afraid and thinking back I was never given anything I could not handle. I accepted what happened as a natural part of my everyday life and as time passed, I learned to read and trust these happenings as naturally as breathing.

The woods and forests were my playground, in the daytime by the light of the Sun and at night time by the light of the Moon. Day or night, they were one and the same to me. I was a child of the forest.

***

One morning, in my parents' house, I awoke as usual to the sound of crashing Lego bricks as another skyscraper fell to the floor. My brothers were always awake before me and I could hear them playing in their bedroom. I slipped out of the cosy warmth of my bed, put my slippers on, grabbed my tiny tears doll and headed to the boys' room to take them down to breakfast.

Even before I entered the kitchen I knew something was wrong. I could see my father standing by the cooker stirring the porridge. He turned and looked at me just for a second and instead of the usual happy morning greeting and big hugs for us all, he merely proceeded to serve the porridge into the breakfast bowls and asked us to sit up to the table. He turned away from us, but not before I noticed how pale and tired he looked and I spotted a hanky hanging out of his trouser pocket. There was none of the usual sparkle in his eyes and no mischievous grin upon his lips. Dad was home at breakfast time, this was all wrong, where was Mum?

As we settled down to eat our breakfast dad broke the news to us that mum had gone away and he did not know when she would be back. In the meantime, to help Dad out so he could continue working, I was to go and stay with Nan and Grandad and a neighbour would be looking after the boys until Dad got home from work each evening.

I was eight years old and my brothers were five and three, they were babies and I felt their hurt, but I didn't know what to do. I was devastated, firstly because I wanted to ask so many questions, but knew this was not the time to do so and secondly, because I did not want to leave my Dad and brothers. I could not understand why they all got to stay together and I was being shipped out, even if it was to my beloved Grandparents. Had I done something wrong, is that why mum had gone and now I had to go too? It felt like I was being punished and I had no idea why.

The weeks rolled into months and although I was very well cared for by Nan and Grandad, I missed my Dad and brothers terribly. I could not understand why they did not come to take me home. I must have been very bad. They did come to visit me though, every Sunday afternoon.

I counted down each day of the week until Sunday morning finally arrived and I knew later that day, Dad's car would come rolling down the lane with my brothers' heads leaning out of the windows waving frantically. I was always up extra early on Sunday mornings, Sunday was visit day and I never strayed far from the house. The morning always seemed to pass so slowly and I watched the clock like no other day of the week willing the hands to move faster. I longed to see dad and the boys and hear all their news I missed them so much, I even missed how they smelt.

The visits seemed to take forever to arrive each week and were always over far too quickly, before we knew it Dad was calling the boys back to the car and we were parted once again. Perhaps next time they would take me home with them. Every Sunday afternoon as I waved goodbye, another little piece of me fell apart.

One afternoon a distant aunt came to visit, she appeared to be very concerned for my wellbeing, I was surprised, I hardly knew her. I was ushered into the lounge with a glass of milk and a biscuit whilst Nan and my aunt entered into a hushed conversation. Even though they tried to talk quietly, I could still hear what they were saying. Apparently, my mother was not coming back, she had run off with a friend of my father's and my poor Dad was beside himself with worry.

At that moment, I felt a pain and fear that I have never forgotten, but I was far too young to know what to do with it so I filed it away in a cupboard deep within my mind. One thing I did know, from now on I would take care of Dad and my brothers and nothing and no one would ever make me leave them again. How wrong I was.

Shortly after my aunt's visit Nan and Grandad called me into the sitting room and told me they had some very good news for me. I was going home. Dad had found someone to come and look after us and we could all be together again as a family. At last I was going home.

Over the next few days Nan busied herself getting all my bits and pieces together, doing my washing and ironing and packing it all away in my little brown suitcase. I collected my books and toys together then carefully packed them in a cardboard box ready to take home with me. We visited the neighbours to say goodbye and then I waited.

The day finally arrived and Dad and the boys were coming to collect me at two-o-clock that afternoon. I sat on the window seat waiting for them from nine-o-clock in the morning, I was so excited.

Eventually, dad's car appeared at the top of the lane and I could not contain myself any longer. I jumped off the seat, out of the house and ran full pelt all the way down the lane to meet them. But, my brothers were not there, the car was eerily still, only Dad had come to get me.

He told me the boys were waiting at home for me and we would be together soon enough. I was so excited to be going home I accepted what I had been told and waited eagerly for the homeward journey.

Dad stopped long enough for a cup of tea and a quick chat with Nan and Grandad then sensing my eagerness to get home, we loaded the boot of the car with my belongings said goodbye to Nan and Grandad and off we went. I told Nan and Grandad not to worry as I stretched up to give them a hug and a kiss goodbye, I would see them as usual at the weekend. I knew they were sad.

As the car pulled away I turned and looked out of the back window waving merrily. I saw Grandad put his arm around Nan's shoulder as she leant in toward him resting her head on his shoulder. He raised an arm to wave me off and I waived back until they were out of sight.

I hold that memory of my Grandfather most dear, for I never saw him again and little did I know it would be many years before I would get to see my Nan.

***

Over the next eight years or so my Magical life took a back seat whilst I studied hard at school and discovered other distractions like boys! I left home just after my sixteenth birthday and went to live in a bedsit. I was free to do as I pleased now and one of the very first things I did was arrange to see my Nan. I wrote to her at the only address I knew, the house where I had spent so much of my early childhood. In the note, I asked her to wait in on a certain day and I would be there.

The day finally arrived and I was going to see my dearest Nan at last, after all these years apart. I pedalled so hard on my bike I thought I might take off, it wouldn't be the first time I thought to myself, but it wasn't a bike I rode on those occasions.

I cycled through the country lanes with my mind a whirl of questions, so many questions until finally, I arrived at Nan's house and was relieved to find it standing exactly as I remembered it from my childhood. I applied the brakes so hard I nearly catapulted myself over the top of the handle bars and as I let go of the bike I heard it hit the ground with a thud and a clatter. I ran to the front door as fast as I could, but before I got there the door opened and there stood Nan.

We fell into each other's arms and cried and laughed and laughed and cried and we did not let go of each other for a very long time. We had so much to talk about, so very much indeed and for the rest of her days on this Earth, that is exactly what we did. We talked and laughed, I listened and I learned.

I didn't have Nan for very long, just a few short years until one Friday afternoon when the phone rang and my blood ran cold. The voice on the other end of the line was telling me Nan was very ill and had been taken into hospital. I dropped everything and rushed to be by her side and that is where I stayed as she slipped further and further away from me and then she was gone.

Although I had not realised it at the time right from as far back as I can remember, Nan had been teaching me the ways of Natural Magic or the Craft, as she liked to call it. She had been preparing me for a way of life that I feel so very privileged and humbled to be part of. A truly Magical existence that is pure and true and teaches respect for every living thing. How lucky am I to have been taught such ways. I live in complete harmony with the rhythm and flow of life, am totally in tune with all that surrounds me and I read life's hidden messages as others read the daily papers.

After Nan died I spent much of my time doing what most people would consider 'normal' things to do, university, work, boyfriends, parties and fun. I became a bit of a rebel if truth be told and got myself involved in all sorts of interesting situations, much of which, I now realise was to do with blocking out my painful past.

I lived life to the full and partied hard, I made acquaintances, not friends, I didn't let anyone get close enough to become my friend. I believed if I didn't let people in to my life then it wouldn't hurt when they left. I was protecting myself. I had a blast, a ball, a great time, but deep down I was empty. I was surrounded by people, the life and soul of any party, but the truth was, I felt completely alone.

Eventually as months melted into years, time passed and before I knew it I was in my thirties and had met and married my wonderful husband, Michael. I had been Blessed to have my brothers and their families in my life and had shared many precious moments with them. Life itself was good, but every now and then around the time of the Full Moon I heard my name being called, riding on the wind like a whisper.

I knew who was calling me, it was my 'other' family, those who were like Nan. I had been away from them for nearly two decades and it was time to go back. I was ready, but I needed to find them first. I knew it would not be easy, people like us can be very difficult to find, we've had to be, so I came up with the brilliant idea of going back to where Nan used to live to look for the copse. If I could find the copse I might be able to find the secret house, the place where we all met.

I decided to start my search. I found the lane where Nan had lived surprisingly easily, my memory served me better than I gave it credit for. My pulse raced and my heart pounded against my chest. It was only now that I was beginning to realise I hadn't actually thought things through very well at all. After all, how nonchalant can you be whilst asking the neighbours if the Witches still worked in the woods?

As I approached the place where the copse had been my heart sank, I couldn't believe what I was looking at. Rows and rows of houses, my beloved grove had gone. A sudden feeling of utter panic flooded through me, oh no, what now? How would I ever find my people? A single sob escaped from deep within me.

I wandered on further up the lane to see if Nan's old house was still standing and to my great relief, found the row of cottages very much the same as I remembered them. I stood outside number 82 and allowed memories to come flooding back to me, such happy times. I was deep in thought when out of nowhere someone called my name.

"I don't believe it look at you all grown up, how are you, got time for a cuppa and a catch up? ".

It was Nan's next door neighbour, old Mr Cutler, he remembered me after all these years. We talked and talked, he always did like to talk and then I heard the words:

"The old house in the copse, do you remember it?" he asked.

Remember it, I had just been trying to find it, but I knew I had to disguise my interest in the place so I played things casually and encouraged him to tell me what he knew. I could not believe what I was hearing.

The land had been bought by a local builder and once things got going on site the houses took shape quickly. However, there was one patch of land that had been left untouched due to the strange goings on every time the builders tried to build on it.

They found the ground kept flooding with water, but there was no spring underground and it wasn't near a stream or a river. The builder had special ground checks done, but no record of a spring or water of any kind nearby could be found. It wasn't long before the workmen refused to go near the site, some said they heard voices calling them others said they felt as if they were being watched. There was a series of unexplained incidents and strange sightings that turned strong burly men into a quivering wreck until eventually, it was decided not to build on the piece of land and it was left as a village green. And the house, the Hidden House, breathed a sigh of relief.

As soon as I politely could, I made my excuses and left, thanking him for his time and hospitality and headed back home. I could hardly contain myself, they were still there I just knew it. All I had to do was wait for when the time was right and then and only then would I return to the green.

As soon as I got home I went straight upstairs to the loft and started to rifle through boxes that I had not looked in for years. I was searching for something very special. I reached in to a large cardboard packing case and proceeded to throw the contents over my shoulder and on to the floor behind me as I emptied it frantically. And then I felt the cool, smooth cover of a silk cloth bag and my heart sang with joy. I had found what I was looking for, my Book of Shadows.

I hurriedly tugged at the ribbon it was bound with, but the knot just would not budge. The more I picked and pulled at it, the tighter the knot seemed to go until out of sheer desperation, I cut the bag open with a pair of scrap book scissors that were lying on an old table nearby. I pulled back the neck of the cloth and removed the precious content.

For a moment or two I just sat and stared at the leather-bound cover so beautifully and intricately decorated. A single tear slid down my cheek as I thought of Nan. I could see her now sat at the table in the bay window of her lounge, only ever:

"On a sunny evening when the light is good", she would say.

I had no idea what she was making at the time, but I knew it made her happy because she sang softly to herself all the while and became totally lost in its creation. I realise now it must have taken her many weeks, probably months to make.

I remember those evenings so clearly and most especially the morning I awoke to find the book at the bottom of my bed. I opened the book excitedly turning its pages one by one to see what secrets and tales they would reveal. But, the pages were totally blank. Nan stood and watched me for a while then began to chuckle to herself before she reached over and took the book back. She told me when I was old enough to know what to do with it, the book would find me and it would be mine. It did and it is.

Slowly opening the front cover to reveal the contents of its pages which by now, many years later, have been well used, I was immediately overcome with emotion. Oh, how I had missed this book, it was like meeting up with an old friend and I felt comforted as I clutched it lovingly to my chest.

It didn't take me too long to familiarise myself with its contents, I knew exactly what I was looking for: a chart for working out the best time to do certain types of magic. It mapped out the correspondences between the Lunar phases and what you wished to achieve.

I needed to know the best time to start searching for the secret house and my people, this was too important to leave to chance. When I found, what I was looking for I set to work and began preparations. Now I knew the right time, my quest could begin and that time was the next New Moon.

As in all things, when waiting for something important or exciting to happen time seems to drag its heels, but wait I had to until at long last the morning of the New Moon arrived. Tonight, was the night I would go back to the site of the copse and look for the tumble down old house, the meeting place. I knew it was still there and I remembered Nan's words;

"Just because we can't see something, doesn't mean it isn't there".

That evening, I arrived at the site of what was now the village green. I stood back for a while watching children play and people walking their dogs until as dusk began to fall, one by one they all disappeared and the place became quiet and still.

I went back to my car opened the boot and got out a robe inherited from my Nan. Robes serve many purposes and on this occasion, it would hide me well from prying eyes. I threw the thick warm material around my shoulders blending easily into the darkness of the night.

I gathered the ribbons at the neck to secure it, pulled up the hood and silently made my way to the village green slipping effortlessly between the houses.

I waited patiently for the last curtain to be drawn and when it felt safe, I moved toward the grassed area to start my search.

I was used to working in the dark, Nan and I had done it often and when your eyes get used to it you can see as if it were daytime. I slowly skirted the edge of the green making absolutely sure no one was about, then edging forward I made my way toward a clump of trees in the centre. I had no idea what I was looking for, but I was being drawn towards a thicket of bushes and brambles. I cursed them quietly for scratching my arms and tangling round my boots and as if in reply, my cloak got caught and I became entangled even further.

I bent down to free myself and tugging frantically at my clothes, fell backward landing flat on my back. I lay there for a while staring at the night sky, not because I had hurt myself, but because I was captured not only by the brambles, but by the beauty of the stars.

Just for a moment I completely forgot where I was or indeed what I was doing there until a mosquito buzzed past my ear bringing me quickly back to the task in hand. Struggling to get up I noticed my hand was resting on something cold and as I looked more closely I could see it was a slab of concrete. No, not a slab, a step, a stone step.

I hurriedly brushed away the leaves and twigs and found another step heading further into the bushes, then another and another and another. I kept going, crawling along on my hands and knees until I came to a wooden post and immediately I knew where I was. The brambles gave way to a clearing and as I stood up by the gatepost I saw a tumble-down cottage and the door of the cottage was slightly open.

It was the house that I had walked past every day as a child with Nan only it wasn't really tumble down at all. This was a house with secrets and it's where the Witches gathered.

I did not hesitate, I simply walked toward the door and pushed it further open. I found my way along the hallway and toward the carved wooden panelling at the side of the staircase. I was looking for the acorn in the carving and when I found it, I pressed the acorn hard and a panel in the staircase tilted open.

I squeezed my way through as I had done so many times before and began to descend the narrow stone staircase. The steps were lit as always by oil lamps hanging from the walls and at the bottom of the steps I followed a well-worn pathway through a tunnel.

As I made my way through the tunnel the familiar heady aroma of incense filled the air welcoming me with each step. I could see the heavy oak door in the distance and as I approached, the door opened and there they were, my Witch family, my friends, I was home.

I awoke the next morning to the sound of bird song filtering through the open bedroom window and as I stretched and yawned lazily, events of the previous night came flooding back to me. I felt a sudden fluttering of butterflies in my stomach and for a moment or two I was consumed by an awful sinking feeling, a feeling of overwhelming panic and disappointment. What if I had not really found the house and my friends after all, what if it had all been just a dream?

As I threw back the quilt to get out of bed I noticed scratch marks all over my legs and arms. Those blooming brambles, so it did happen! I had the scars to prove it, either that or I had been sleep walking. I looked across at the bedside table and there, propped up against my glass of water, was a piece of paper with the venue time and date of our next meeting.

From that day, onward I had a spring in my step, nothing was too much trouble and I sang merrily as I went about my business. I was truly happy and totally fulfilled for the first time in many years. Everyday life continued as usual and no one would ever guess I was a practising Witch.

Surprising as it may be, I do not actually go around the village dressed in long flowing robes and a tall pointy hat, nor am I to be found chanting spells and talking to toads, well not where anyone would ever see me anyway.

I have never felt the need to advertise the fact I am a Witch and over the years I have learned that one way or another the 'Burning Times' are not over. Far from it in fact, they never truly have been and we need to continue to be careful.

I had been out since first light collecting fresh herbs and on the way back to my cottage, I noticed a parcel had been left in the front porch. It was a wicker basket filled with cut flowers, jams and marmalades, home-made cakes and elderflower cordial. There was a message inside which simply read, 'Welcome Home' and I knew who it was from instantly.

I picked up the basket to carry it indoors when a sudden thought occurred to me, I hadn't given anyone my address last night, so how did they know where I lived? The answer of course was, they had known all along where I was, all those years, they had been waiting.

It is a time-honoured tradition of the Craft that we look after our own we always have and we always will and above all else, we trust each other with our lives, literally. We are open and honest with one another and encouraged to ask questions that is how we learn, but sometimes, just sometimes, there is no need to ask anything.

We accept things for what they are and know that all is as it should be and this was most definitely one of those occasions.

During the following days and weeks memories of my Nan came flooding back to me as bit by bit, pieces of the puzzle began to fall into place. All the stories Nan used to tell me as a little girl, afternoons in the woods with Aunt Queenie foraging from the hedgerows, all those hours spent with Grandad in his garden and those precious times in Nan's kitchen making all sorts of concoctions. Now I understood they were so very much more than just fun, they were lessons in the art of the Craft.

Whilst I had been pre-occupied with 'Life' in general and away from the Craft I had moved house several times losing many of my 'Tools of the Trade' in the process. I would have to start gathering the various bits and pieces all over again and those I could not find I would make, for example a willow wand and an altar. As luck, would have it, a friend of mine had recently come across a large ring of oak wood and asked me if I would like it for my wood burner. Like it I most certainly did, but not for the wood burner, my goodness no, that ring of oak was going to be my new altar.

I spent ages sanding down the surfaces of each side to make them smooth and flat then painted Magical symbols on one side and left the other side completely natural to show the beauty of the wood.

Each side was sealed with beeswax and polished to perfection until they shone like glass. A friend of mine who is a blacksmith connected a central pivot of black wrought iron right through the sides and hey presto – a garden table by day and when spun over, an altar by night.

Making my wand and altar was only the beginning. I gathered herbs, flowers, berries, barks and cones and dried them to make incense, I collected candles of all shapes and sizes, crystals came to me as gifts and precious finds and I visited charity shops and the like for candle holders, bells, pots, jars, ribbons and all sorts of other trinkets. Before long I had acquired an enviable collection of working tools and I couldn't wait to start using them.

As the time of the next gathering approached I could hardly contain myself with excitement. I was keen to show the others how hard I had been working and was desperate to Bless my new working tools ready for use.

The site they had chosen for this celebration was unfamiliar to me, but I followed the instructions I had been given and soon arrived at the designated meeting place. I pulled into the lay-by and one of the group members came over and told me to leave my car where it was, we were to travel the rest of the way together in his vehicle. After a short drive, we turned off-road and continued up a dirt track well worn by heavy tyres.

The ride was bumpy to say the least and when the jeep finally pulled to a halt I was beginning to wish I hadn't eaten quite so much supper. We trudged along on foot for some time in the cold night air and I was loving every minute of it. Familiar smells of the forest filled my nostrils as I inhaled deeply; green moss, fungi, damp leaves, rotting wood and pine needles. As we walked along I heard the occasional 'snap' of twigs being broken alongside us, we were not alone. Other creatures of the night were following us curiously.

Eventually we spotted the amber glow of a campfire like a beacon guiding us in. We approached the Circle, no one spoke they simply nodded and gestured where I was to stand. I could just about make out the smiles from underneath the hoods of their ceremonial robes and I felt their silent welcome as warmly as the heat coming from the campfire.

The ground was struck with three determined blows from a heavy willow staff and the ritual began.

The High Priest and High Priestess performed the Blessing of the Altar invoked the quarters and cast the circle ready for working. I noticed the area around us had been lovingly created from a selection of nearby fallen twigs and branches, each one laid carefully to form a perfect Circle of protection. Tiny white tea lights flickered and danced playfully their presence adding to the atmosphere.

The altar had been set with the basic items as usual and complimented with white and silver ribbons, white flowers and candles. The altar of a New Moon is often set this way and is a reflection of its deeper meanings. The colour white, represents new hopes, new beginnings and purity and the colour silver represents the Lunar metal of silver for divine feminine energy.

After the initial opening ceremony and wishes had been done it was time to ask the Coven members if they had any specific New Moon workings they wished to do. Those who did came to the centre of the Circle and performed their rituals. Wherever necessary, members of the group gave willingly of their strength and energy to enhance any Magic being done and achieve goals being set. New Moon is a time for healing, bringing renewed good health and strength to those who may need it. It is a time for new beginnings in all things such as starting new ventures or new relationships. Those who are creative often find they have an abundance of new ideas or spurt of creativity and energy during this time.

The New Moon heralds ever increasing strength and spirituality as She creeps ever nearer to Her climax and her Fullness. It is for this reason that spells and magical workings done during the period between a New Moon and a Full Moon often focus on harnessing the energies present during this phase to culminate in release on the next Full Moon.

Once everyone had finished their ritual, it was my turn. I asked if I could have my new working tools cleansed and Blessed. Each item was passed through the four elements of earth, air, fire and water and then offered up to the Goddess for her Blessing.

When everything had been cleansed and Blessed appropriately they were returned to me. I was ecstatic, my working tools were ready to be used and I couldn't wait to get started.

As the ritual ended we removed our robes and began packing everything away chatting and laughing as usual at some tale or another. The time after a ritual is an opportunity for socialising and much merriment, a time to relax and enjoy each other's company. It was during this time that I was called to one side by the High Priest. We sat together on a nearby tree trunk just slightly away from the others and he asked if I was glad to be back and I assured him I was. He looked deep into my eyes, into my soul and then he said:

"Are you ready?"

I knew what he meant and without hesitation I told him that I most certainly was. He smiled a gentle knowing smile and said he was pleased to hear it.

Nan had explained to me as a young girl that when the time was right I would be given the opportunity to learn more of all things magical. She told me I must never ask and would have to wait until I was approached by the right person. Despite my many protests and questions such as, how would I know who this person was and how long would I have to wait and so on, she never once gave in, but simply replied;

"When the student is ready, the Master will appear and you will know". This was the time and I knew it.

We returned to the others and the High Priest asked for silence, he spoke of his invitation to me and asked for their agreement. The vote had to be unanimous, every member of the coven would have to give an 'Aye' or it simply did not happen and my journey in the Craft stopped there. I don't know why, but I held my breath as one by one they gave their answers. What if someone objected, what would I do then? I couldn't bear it if anyone objected and just as I was about to faint due to lack of oxygen from holding my breath so long, the final 'Aye' was given. They had all agreed, it was done.

For the next thirteen Moons I would study with an Elder and learn all I could about the Craft, its Magic, ceremonies and rituals and if, at the end of that time all had gone well, I would be initiated as a Witch of the First Degree. I looked up to the sky and hoped Nan was watching, she would be so proud of me. I floated home that night, my mind full of wonder and excitement, I had so many questions to ask and plans to make and for days I couldn't stop smiling. People kept asking me what I had been up to and when were they going to meet him! If only they knew what I was so happy about.

My involvement with the Craft till now had only ever been what I had learned from Nan and attendance at open celebrations. These events are very different to ritual magic. When we celebrate openly anyone may be invited to attend, we are not performing magic of any kind, we are celebrating cyclical events such as; New Moon, Full Moon, Solstice, Yule, Beltaine, Imbolc, Lughnasadh and Samhain.

These are phases of the Moon and various festivals throughout the year which celebrate and mark the changing of the seasons and the turning of the Wheel of Life.

To be invited to work with an Elder and study magic is something completely different and a great honour. An Elder is a person who is an experienced Witch, usually an older person although not necessarily, the term Elder is used purely out of respect. You cannot ask to be trained in this way, traditionally you must wait to be asked to join a Circle. Circle magic is for those who know and is not discussed in the outside world.

I so wanted to announce to the world that I was a 'Witch in Training', but I knew I must not utter a word, it was hard not being able to speak of such things, I was so excited. Instead, I bought every book I could find about the Craft and immersed myself in a reading frenzy. I wanted to impress them, but the more I read the more I became confused and at times alarmed at what I was reading. Much of it was basic enough and would do well to answer the enquiring mind of someone who was just curious. Some of it in my opinion, showed little respect for the Craft and its traditions and simply confuses true Witch–Crafting with nothing more than sensationalism.

Others I feel told too much and some served only to bring discredit and dishonour to the table. Mud sticks and that has been and I guess always will be the problem, so I stopped all the reading and decided to wait and see and make up my own mind.

To the outside world, I did not look any different, but on the inside I felt very different. It was a strange feeling, like I had a big sign stamped across my forehead, 'Witch'. I was convinced everyone was looking at me and knew what I was doing.

Part of me found it exciting, part of me felt a little uneasy, I don't know why. Perhaps it was in recognition of the fear of persecution we had experienced in times gone by, perhaps I was 'remembering'. Either way, it served me well and reminded me to be cautious about speaking to people about my way of life and as it turned out, there would be very few people who would ever get to know.

My day to day life continued as normal, but with each passing Moon and the teachings that came with Her, I became totally immersed and very happily absorbed in learning all I could about my Craft. It has been an amazing journey and there are so many tales to tell, so I will start with them as I remember them, one by one.

# Part Two – Falling Moon

It had been a quiet morning in my pottery and I was working in the shop glazing my latest creation. The door opened and in came a young woman, slight of build with the most stunning flame red hair cascading down her back in a most unruly manner. I knew instantly.

"Wow!", she said, "you must have been my sister in another life, look, we've got matching hair". I knew from those first few words we would become friends, little did I know just how important this person was to become in my life and what an incredible journey we were about to embark upon.

From our conversation that morning I had learned much about her, she was interested in all things nature based, mystical and magical and knew much about astrology.

She bought some crystals, a book and some incense and as she reached over the counter to pay, I saw a ring on her finger, a silver pentacle. The Craft had not been mentioned so I made no comment, bid her good day and looked forward to our next meeting. I did not have to wait long, just hours in fact. She called me that very evening and we arranged to meet the following week. It wasn't until we had put the phone down that I realised we were meeting on a New Moon, of course we were.

Claire arrived at my house on time and in good spirits and it was not long before she asked me outright.

"Well then, are you going to tell me or do I have to guess? Solitary or coven?" she asked. From that moment on a very special friendship was forged that lasts to this day and one which will always have a special place in my heart.

We spent the rest of that evening planning a ritual for the next Full Moon. I had worked many times in the garden on my own, it was well sheltered from prying eyes and my husband had created a beautiful area he refers to as the 'Witch zone'. It is a well concealed and private place for me to work, complete with my own altar, statues, wind chimes, mirrors, running water and crystals, he has even built into the walls an area for the candles to be placed so they don't blow out on a windy night. I love it.

The night of the Full Moon arrived and so did Claire and together we set the altar and prepared for ritual. After the opening ceremony, we sat on the grass and were chatting quite happily, when I happened to look up at the Moon. I couldn't help but gasp out loud as the Moon appeared to come hurtling toward us. The sensation sent me reeling to one side and I grabbed hold of Claire's arm for support.

"What on earth was that?" asked Claire in utter astonishment as we both stared upward in total disbelief. She had seen it too.

"Nearly the Moon", I replied somewhat dryly and for several moments we both sat transfixed and speechless staring into space.

Something had clearly just happened, but neither of us had any idea exactly what that might be. We helped each other up and began to take down the Circle when out of the corner of my eye, over by the apple tree I saw something walk past us. It was a Wolf, a most magnificent silver grey wolf with black markings, almost as big as me. It stopped, turned its head toward us and looked straight at me. I was captivated, thoroughly entranced allowing myself the sheer pleasure of falling into its steely grey eyes.

During the next few seconds something very odd occurred, it was as though some kind of energy transference was taking place. I felt a strange buzzing sensation course its way through my body and was immediately consumed with visions and feelings I have no way of explaining. I was feeling nauseous and giddy, but as quickly as it had started, it stopped and that was that.

Claire continued packing away the altar completely oblivious of our visitor as magnificent as he was, or of what was happening to me. I decided not say anything, it was our first time working together and I really didn't want to totally freak her out.

One lot of excitement was enough for now and after all, hadn't we just witnessed the Moon 'falling' from the sky?

We went indoors to make ourselves a hot drink and talk about what happened, but neither of us had any idea what to make of it. We decided the best thing to do was find out as much as we could and report back to each other later.

I went to bed that night full of questions going over and over the night's events. Did that all really happen, could we have imagined it, did I really have a wolf in my back garden, what if he had escaped from somewhere, had the Moon really fallen from the sky?

I lay back on my bed and fell into a very deep sleep.

The following weeks passed normally and when I wasn't busy working I spent any spare time I had trying to find answers to the questions about what happened the other night during the ritual with Claire.

You may well be wondering why I just didn't ask one of the Elders. The answer is simple, I was being taught the 'Old Ways' in the traditional manner. It is the way things are sometimes done and considered to be part of the learning experience. We are encouraged as neophytes 'new ones' or 'Witch in the making' to do much of the learning on our own, to forge new friendships and acquaintances and be as independent of the coven as much as possible. The Elders are always there for us, but during the first year of learning we see very little of them. We are encouraged to make our own way along the path of the Craft and it is considered a test of commitment and boy oh boy, have I been tested!

After several months of working on our own Claire and I decided it would be nice to join a group of like-minded people with whom we could share our experiences and learn from each other.

We were already aware of a well-known pagan organisation and once initial contact had been made and we had gone through the introductory stages, we were given the time, date and address of the next local moot. A 'moot' is the term used to describe a 'meeting place'.

We were very excited to be joining a group, but had no idea what to expect, our imagination was working overtime. By the time, we arrived at the venue we had decided everyone was sure to be wearing cloaks, carrying a black cat and sporting big pointy hats. And the broomsticks, oh yes, the broomsticks, well, they of course would all be lined up in an orderly fashion outside the front of the pub! Wouldn't they?

Important lesson – never judge a book by its cover, not even a Spell Book. The meeting place turned out to be a quintessentially English country pub, very quaint, very pretty and not a broomstick in sight. We parked the car and rather cautiously made our way into the pub.

Everyone and everything looked so normal, people were drinking and chatting and having a good time and almost immediately we began to question if this was indeed the right place. No one appeared to take any notice of us at all and carried on their conversations as if we were invisible.

I don't quite know what we were expecting, but strangely enough it wasn't this. We ordered a drink and sat down watching and listening in case anyone, anywhere gave us the slightest inkling they were part of the moot.

No one did and nothing happened, so we just sat there wondering what to do next. Eventually, we concluded we were in the wrong place and had just decided to finish our drink and leave, when a man from behind the bar called us over.

"You two part of the pointy hat brigade then? Coz if so, they're all upstairs, come on through, I'll take you up ".

Claire and I looked at each other puzzled to the say the least, how did he know? did we have 'Witches' tattooed on our foreheads?

We were taken through the bar to the back of the pub and led up a narrow winding staircase. At the top of the stairs was a heavy wooden latch-door, the man knocked on the door three times then pushed it open slowly.

"Some new'uns for ya", he announced to the room as we entered and a sea of smiling faces turned toward us. Several people got up and came over to greet us. I liked these people straight away they were kind and welcoming and immediately made us feel at ease. They were in the middle of a talk by a New Forest verderer so we settled quickly, made our apologies for disturbing them and listened with interest to the rest of the session.

When the talk was over a tall young woman came over to our table and introduced herself. She was the person who had sent us the instructions on when and where to meet. We chatted for quite a while and she asked what had brought us to contact the organisation in the first place. I knew however much she might fall off her chair laughing, I just had to tell her about my experience with the wolf and the Moon. She did not laugh instead she listened intently then nodded and asked us to wait there.

She returned some while later with a much older lady who had the kindest, greenest eyes I have ever seen and a youthfulness about her that belied her years. The older lady asked if I would mind repeating the story about the wolf and the Moon. At the end of the tale she sat back in her chair deep in thought, then said,

"So, you're an Old Soul are you".

I puzzled at her words, 'Old Soul', what did she mean?

"Forgive me" I said, "I don't understand what you."

"I know you don't my dear, she replied, but you will, in time, you will".

As she got up to leave she spoke to the young woman who had come to greet us in the first place. They looked over to where Claire and I were sat, smiled politely then went about their business.

For the rest of the evening we mingled happily and I noticed a comforting sense of calmness and kindness about the place. The evening passed by quickly and before we knew it people were saying their goodbyes. We turned to make our way down the stairs when a member of the group came over and asked if we would like to come to the next meeting. We told them we most certainly would and with that they asked for our telephone numbers and said we would hear from them soon.

All the way home that night Claire and I chatted excitedly about who we had met, what we had observed, what we had been told and what we had overheard.

They were a mixed bunch of people that's for sure and came from all sorts of backgrounds including a teacher, solicitor, doctor, refuse collector and a window cleaner and we could not wait to meet them all again.

When the details of the next meeting came through we were surprised to find it was a private address, but neither of us gave it much thought and on that evening, we drove to the address we had been given and rang the front door bell.

The loudness of the chimes startled us somewhat as they rang out their cheerful tune and we nearly missed the gentle voice from within, calling out softly for us to enter. Pushing the front door open we followed the sound of the voice and made our way toward a room at the back of the cottage.

We were greeted by the elderly lady we had met at the moot and I must admit, I felt a sense of relief. She was sat in a rocking chair by the fire and as we entered the room she held her hand out to greet us. The moment I took her hand I felt something like an electric shock shoot all the way up my arm, we looked at each other, but neither one of us said anything. She asked Claire and I to sit down and make ourselves comfortable.

"So, I guess you want to know why you are here then" she said and we both nodded eagerly in agreement.

"Well, it all has to do with what you told me at the moot the other evening about the wolf and the Moon falling from the sky. Let me explain

***

For the next hour or so Claire and I sat transfixed, hanging on her every word. We could hardly believe what we were hearing, but then again who would?

She told us that the Moon appearing to fall toward us was the beginning of a very sacred journey for us both. The Moon Goddess had presented herself by quite literally, 'falling to Earth'. It was an invitation for us to follow in Her path, the path of the Craft. The presence of the Wolf signified Divine feminine energy and was a symbol of protection. He had appeared not only to watch over and protect us, but in confirmation that what happened that night was real and ours for the taking. We were told experiences like these usually only occurred to those who were already a Witch and had been for many lifetimes.

She explained in detail exactly what would be involved if we chose to follow the path of the Craft and by the time she had finished, we had been left in no doubt as to the level of commitment this would require. Having been given a short while to reflect on what we had been told, we were asked us if this was what we had been seeking and without hesitation we both said yes.

"In that case and just for you, I will come out of retirement", she declared.

"I will take you both on for exactly one year and one day. But, take note, the path of the Craft will not always be an easy one, you will be tested every step of the way and sometimes to your absolute limit. You come when you are called and you do not question an instruction. Now, having said all this, are you sure you want to go ahead?"

Claire and I nodded eagerly in unison.

"Well then, better see what you're made of", she declared.

"See that box of matches on the coffee table over there, I want you to concentrate really hard, stay focussed and see if you can move it to any other place on the table".

Claire and I sat there motionless staring at the box willing it to move with all our might. We could not fail our first test, we had to impress this woman, come on box, move. There was complete silence in the room you could have heard a pin drop, but try as we might the box just would not move.

After a few minutes or so our mentor got up from her chair, went over to the table, picked up the box and put it on the mantelpiece.

Claire and I looked at her in utter disbelief then looked at each other completely bemused.

"I asked you to move the box, I did not say you could not touch it. By carefully selecting my words I could influence your thought process without you even realising it. In this case, the word was 'concentrate'. You immediately and quite naturally associated the word with the mind and from that moment onward you made your own assumptions. In fact, you did not listen at all to what I asked you to do, you simply did what you 'thought' I had asked you to do and that is a very different matter".

I think at that point Claire and I felt a mixture of foolishness and embarrassment at having failed our very first task. Whatever would she make of us now? We needn't have worried, she returned to her chair chortling to herself heartily and with a triumphant air about her declared,

"Here endeth the first lesson. I can see we are going to have much fun during our journey together and I'm already looking forward to our next lesson. Go now, I am getting tired, we shall meet again in exactly four weeks' time".

As we were getting ready to leave I went over to say thank you and shake her hand. As I did so, she pulled me toward her and said, "My name is Molly by the way and I am very pleased to meet you, I've been waiting for you for a very long time."

Our lessons with Molly continued each month for about a year or so and we became regulars at the local moots. We joined in open rituals and celebrated the New Moon and the Full Moon, the Solstices and Equinoxes, the camps and everything in between and we loved every minute. We learned how to make our own wands, robes and cloaks, the art of meditation and journeying, how to scry (an old term used to describe the art of reading cards and stones, crystals and sticks). We were shown how to read a crystal ball and make a 'Witches Mirror' and of course, quite naturally, we were taught how to make a spell.

We sang and danced and laughed and all the time we were learning. The more I learned the more I remembered and like the pieces of a jig saw puzzle, the picture began to grow and I began to understand my past.

I thought about the times as a little girl when I was on my own, but not on my own, playing with children and animals that no one else could see. It wasn't so much a physical presence, they appeared in a more transparent form. I could see straight through them, but they were there and we played for hours. I was never frightened and I missed them when they didn't come. There were many times when I would wish and wish for them to appear calling out as I searched in cupboards, rooms, the garden shed, the old air raid shelter, the cellar, anywhere I thought they might be hiding.

They never came to order, they only ever came when they wanted to. I could be indoors playing happily on my own or down in the field picking flowers, one minute I was on my own and the next, there they were. As I grew older the children came less and less, but the animals have stayed with me always and are frequent visitors when I am in Circle or working with patient's in my herbal clinic. Some may say the children were a figment of my childhood imagination. My answer to that is; they may well have been, but how many times do you know of people's 'imaginations', leaving them little gifts? My little friends did, quite often. I remember one occasion I shall never forget.

It was a beautiful summer's day, in fact it was Midsummer's Eve. I remember this because Nan and I had been up early that morning collecting dew as it hung upon the grass like sparkling diamonds. We tapped each blade of grass gently with little sticks until the dew drop fell into tiny glass phials. When we had collected enough, the phials were sealed shut with the tiniest of cork stoppers and stored in a big ceramic jar Nan used to keep the milk cool. I didn't know it then, but Nan was preparing a Mid-Summer spell to help her 'See' the Faerie Folk during celebrations she would be part of later that night.

Anyway, back to my tale. Later that day I decided to take myself off to the bottom of the garden and clamber through a hole in the hedge leading out into the field beyond. I was walking along the hedgerow looking for bird's nests, when I noticed movement off to the side of me and some way into the field. Grandad told me never to go into the field alone and I was mindful of his words, but I had a feeling something was wrong so I ignored his advice and made my way across the field. I followed the commotion that was going on and came upon a blackbird with its leg trapped in some plastic wire. I slowly bent toward the bird and speaking in a gentle voice I managed to calm the bird and free its leg.

It must have been exhausted because it didn't fly away, it just sat there so I sat down on the grass beside it and stroked its silken feathers. I don't know if it was the heat of the day or the fact that I had not long had lunch, but I must have drifted off to sleep because the next thing I knew, I was waking up to the gentle hum of a bumble bee, or so I thought.

In my dozy state, I struggled to sit myself up and began to look round for the bird, but the bird had flown away and I was pleased because it meant it was alright. I rubbed my sleepy eyes to wake myself up properly and as I did so was delighted to find my friends had come to join me. I immediately began telling them all about the bird, but no one seemed in the slightest bit interested.

Then I noticed something most odd, they were sat in a complete circle all around me, heads bent downward, eyes closed and holding hands. I spoke to them again, but they seemed to be ignoring me, so I stood up, walked straight past them and made my way back through the hedge and up to the house.

That evening Grandad came in from the garden and told Nan he had been chatting to the farmer who was working in the field at the bottom of the garden. The farmer had been telling Grandad about a strange event that had taken place that afternoon.

Apparently, the farmer had been busy cutting corn all day, but every time he got near one corner of the field, the tractor engine stopped. After several attempts to get it going he gave up and went back to the farmhouse for some tools. On his return to the tractor he could not believe what he was **seeing**. Right in front of where the tractor had stopped was a perfectly formed circle of flattened corn.

"Come on Ivy", said Grandad, "come and have a look, it's still there, looks just like one of them crop circle things". So, we all went out to the field to see what everyone was getting so excited about and there it was, a perfect circle surrounding the exact spot where I had fallen asleep with the bird. That day, my friends gave me the most precious gift, the gift of life.

Nan's garden was not just beautiful to look at, it served as her larder and her medicine chest. I watched each morning as she strolled around the garden stopping here and there to smell and touch each plant as it grew. Then, when the time was just right, she would lovingly and tenderly harvest just what she needed to replenish her stores of natural remedies. When the herbs and flowers had been collected, they were tied into small bunches with nettle twine and hung up to dry.

They hung from every available space we could find, from the Lazy Susan that hung over the Aga, to cupboard door handles until eventually the whole place looked like a woodland grotto, it was magical.

We dried sage leaves ready to treat ailments of the throat, elderberries and rosehips to ward off winter coughs and colds, lavender flowers to ease symptoms of anxiety and mint leaves for digestive upsets. I especially liked the lip salves Nan made using honey and beeswax, they evoked a sense of comfort and tranquillity about the place and I found the aroma soothing to the mind. Nan was harnessing the powers of Nature to make natural medicines and I marvelled at her unwritten skills and knowledge. She was the village healer, the village Wise Woman.

I recalled the times I watched Nan from my bedroom window late at night slipping silently from the house her dark cloak billowing out behind her as she disappeared into the night. I sat on the windowsill and tried to wait up for her every time, but always awoke the next morning tucked up in my bed safe and sound. I knew when I went downstairs for breakfast there would be a cloak and a velvet bag hung up on the back of the scullery door and a pair of black lace up boots tucked underneath them on the floor.

Breakfast time lasted for ages on these occasions as I stared in obvious puzzlement at the intriguing sights before me, instead of eating my cereals. Nan carried on with her household chores pretending not to notice my curiosity and each time I asked who's cloak and boots they were I received the same reply.

"Do you know what inquisitive means?" she would say.

I replied I did not.

"Well then, when you know what it means and can spell it, I will tell you the answer to your question".

I knew by lunchtime the items would be gone - until the next time.

Then there were the times during the evening of each New Moon when Nan took her purse out into the garden to turn over each silver coin she had in it.

I remember from a very early age, especially during winter months when the days drew shorter, going out into the garden with her, clutching my own tiny purse. I turned my silver coins over too. She told me this would make sure we always had enough money and our purses would never be empty.

"All we ever need, is just enough", she would say.

I had no idea at the time just how profound this simple statement was.

I giggle to myself even now, when I think of the times I was tempted to say or do something I knew I probably shouldn't and from nowhere Nan would appear and say to me;

"Well littl'un, it's up to you, but if you want that broom over there to turn around and chase you all the way up the lane……." and I would reply most indignantly,

"Brooms can't chase me, they can't move".

"That one can", said Nan and now I know, it probably could.

It was one of the very first things Claire and I had learned about with Molly, the Witches broom, correctly referred to as a 'besom'. In the olden days when it was not safe to openly practice 'Moon' magic in any form, Witches carried out rituals using an up-turned kitchen broom as their altar. It's quite easy to hang bits and pieces from the twigs and use them to hold things in place. If anyone came knocking at the door unexpectedly all you had to do was kick the handle of the broom with your foot, everything fell to the floor and 'hey presto', no altar, just mess everywhere, very like the floor of any busy household really.

There were other things to be learnt about the besom, but they came later. The more I remembered the more I began to realise without a shadow of a doubt; my Nan was a Witch.

As time went on and weeks turned into months working with the Craft became as natural to me as breathing. More and more l was caught out by the feeling I had done this all before and found my instincts and intuition developing rapidly. I began to know or sense certain things, for example; visiting places I had never been to before and yet when we got there I knew exactly where I was. I could describe local buildings, places and even the local landscape, it became a bit of a party piece over the years.

The strange thing was I rarely remembered the places as they were in the present day, instead I saw them as bygone times. I recognised this fact because of the way people were dressed and the way they spoke, the noises and the smells, but often the landscape and buildings had remained unchanged even over time.

There was however another side to all this personal development that I found difficult to master and sometimes still do. I began to 'sense' things about people that were not always what one would wish to know.

The first time it happened I was at the checkout queue in my local supermarket. I was patiently waiting my turn as you do when I happened to glance across to another aisle and saw a man packing away his shopping. Nothing unusual there then except just for a moment, right around the abdominal area of his body I saw a dark cloud then as clear as clear could be, the cloud changed shape to that of a human liver and I knew he was unwell.

I did not know exactly what was wrong with him, but I knew his liver was in trouble. I could not believe what had just happened so, I looked around at other people in the store, but thank goodness nothing else odd was happening to them. My first instinct was to go over and speak with him about what had just occurred, after all I am a fully qualified nurse and medical practitioner, I might be able to help in some way, but you can't do that to a total stranger can you? I mean really, can you imagine what might have happened?

Happenings such as these became a regular occurrence, anytime, anywhere, they just happened. Someone could pass me by in the street and suddenly I would feel an ache in my back and I knew they had back problems. One afternoon a young boy rode past me on his bike and I felt a sudden shortness of breath.

I turned to watch him as he cycled along the path when suddenly, he fell off his bike. I ran over to help him and found he was basically alright and not hurt in any way, but he appeared to be gasping for air. He pointed to his jacket which had been draped over the handlebars of the bicycle, I reached over and passed it to him. From one of the pockets he withdrew an inhaler and within a few puffs he was breathing much easier and became calm. The shock of the fall had bought on an asthma attack and I had experienced his discomfort before it had even happened.

As these occurrences began to increase in frequency I decided to ask Molly what was happening and if she could explain what was going on. She told me my Third eye chakra was opening.

The Third eye in psycho-therapeutic terms is an area located in between the eyes at the centre of the forehead. It is the energy centre of spiritual awareness, creativity and psychic ability. When these energy centres are activated or stimulated in some way we become more connected and open to receiving information from our surroundings. Molly suggested this was what was happening to me.

Molly asked if I was frightened by what had been happening and I told her that I was not actually frightened by it, but I did find it disconcerting at times. She chuckled to herself,

"My, that's a big word, swallowed a dictionary for breakfast 'av we?".

I smiled at her comment, I was getting used to her sense of humour, it's something all Witches have in abundance. When you are on your way to a ritual trapesing through forests in the dead of night, knee deep in mud, hailstones stinging your face from the lashing rain and you can't see your hand in front of your face, you have to have a sense of humour.

"Thing is", said Molly, "not to let these visions become troublesome, which they will if you do not learn to control them. It is very easy to become so engrossed in other worldly goings on shall we say, that you forget you are living in this time and this place. You must learn to control these thoughts and not let them control you". With Molly's help and guidance Claire and I learnt how to do just that.

It was all about learning to make the conscious decision how and when we would allow such information to come through. It was a bit like learning to activate an on/off button, but most importantly we must always be in control.

I will never forget the time Molly set Claire and I a task specifically aimed at demonstrating the inter-connectedness between the human mind and Universal energy. She asked us to think of something totally bizarre that we wanted to happen as a sign of proof that thoughts were living things. The exercise was to demonstrate how our thoughts really could become solid evidence of another dimension at work.

We were to report back at our next meeting and just before we left that night she told us we must set a time frame for it to happen. We agreed whatever our challenge was to be, it had to happen in the next four weeks.

Claire and I chatted about our challenges all the way home that night. We decided to really test this theory to its limits so instead of going for the usual run of the mill – think of someone and see if they phone you type scenario, we chose very specific tasks for the Universe to act upon.

Claire decided she wanted to see yellow balloons stuck in a hedge which would be quite something because the chances are if balloons got stuck in a hedge they would probably pop; I decided upon white feathers to show themselves in a way that could leave absolutely no doubt in my mind. We set the challenges there and then on our way home in the car. Job done, now all we had to do was wait and see if the Universe had been listening.

The remaining journey home was strangely quiet, I think both of us felt a little uneasy at what we had just done. Think about it for a moment and you will soon realise the implications of such actions. Could we really influence things to happen just by 'putting it out there'? The whole concept and possible consequences of this task were almost mind blowing and I think we both realised the potential of what we had done. What if it worked?

We would find out, just three days later.

Claire decided to go north to visit a friend she had not seen for years and not being a lover of motorway driving she had decided to go the 'pretty way' via old country roads. Having lost her way numerous times, she was once again pulled up in a lay-by, fighting with the map and wondering why they were always twice the size of the front of the car. No way could you ever locate the place you were looking for without opening the map fully, then it engulfed you completely like a giant marshmallow.

Having got into a right muddle she slammed the map down into her lap with a huge 'Hurrrumpff' then froze in an instant. Recalling the events that followed she remembered how an eerie chill ran through her body as she felt the colour drain from her face. Gasping out loud and pointing a finger in the direction of the front wind screen, there in the hedgerow, right in front of the car waving in the breeze, was a bunch of yellow balloons.

She slowly reached across the passenger seat to retrieve her mobile phone and took a photo. She remembers the odd feeling that everything she was doing had to be in slow motion in case any sudden movement would cause the spectacle in front of her to pop and be gone. Nothing 'popped' and nothing disappeared and within seconds I had received the image on my mobile, just as I was sending her a photo of what I was looking at…

That day, I had been busy with patients in clinic all morning and as I waved the last one goodbye, my tummy rumbled and I decided it was time to stop for lunch. I closed the clinic door and made my way out into the kitchen on the hunt for something not too fattening for lunch. I looked out of the kitchen window, grabbed an apple out of the fruit bowl and turned toward the fridge, now what else shall I have I mused to myself?

I bent to open the fridge door then stopped in my tracks, turned back toward the window and promptly dropped the apple. I could not believe what I was seeing, so I hurried to the back door went out through the porch and stood there halted in total disbelief at what lay before me. It was a carpet of beautiful pure white feathers strewn from one end of the garden to the other, all 150 feet of it. I could not believe my eyes, I had never seen anything like it before and I doubt I ever will again, but right here and right now my garden was absolutely covered in white feathers.

I did not know what to do next, should I go indoors and get the camera, I had to get a picture, how else would I be able to prove this had happened

If I moved would it all vanish in a puff of smoke like magic, for this really was magic. I have no idea why I did what I did next, but I began to walk slowly backwards into my kitchen through the cottage and into my office where I grabbed my mobile phone. I then crept, yes crept slowly back out into the garden almost too afraid to look because surely this was not happening?

It was and the feathers were still there so I took the photos to prove it and in a click I had sent them to Claire with the message:

'You are not going to believe what has just happened here'.

To which I got the reply:

'Oh, yes I would' as a photo of her yellow balloons stuck in a hedge pinged through to me. I gasped out loud and was silent. What the hell had we done?

I vowed from that moment I would never feel the need to challenge the Universe again and I never have. I accepted what had occurred was far more than just a lesson set by our mentor and delivered by the Universe. This was a glimpse of the infinite possibilities that were opening up to us as students of the Craft and amongst the messages it portrayed came the realisation that this was most serious and certainly not a game..

For the first time ever, I felt the heaviness of the burden of responsibility such knowledge and power brings with it.

Over the years there have been many occasions when I have had cause to remember those early feelings of apprehension. The Craft is most certainly not for everyone, not because it is in any way bad or evil, but because it is so very powerful.

I have learned that all life is connected, like the weave of a spider's web. If you are sad, I am sad, if you are happy, I am happy. In all life, there is dark and there is light, good and bad and when you understand how delicately everything is balanced and how easy it is to disrupt the status quo, then you hold the key to Pandora's box. This is a far too heavy load for many to bear.

***

Our journey with Molly lasted exactly thirteen Moons and was a unique blend of serious teachings, fun and laughter, camps and gatherings. One month drifted into another, the seasons passed, the wheel turned and the cycle of life continued as it always has.

Having successfully completed our first year of training, Claire and I knew it would not be long before we were asked if we wished to proceed with Initiation to the First Degree. This is a huge step for anyone to take and when done properly demands much careful consideration and preparation. At no time are we ever forced or persuaded in any way what to do, the decision is entirely ours and is taken in our own time.

Throughout my studies with Molly, I had grown to realise that initiation to the First Degree was so much more than just dressing up, having fun and being able to perform rituals and ceremonies. It was much deeper and more complex than that. You must learn and agree to abide by, Craft Law – yes, we do live by certain Laws and all that they entail. It is about learning to accept responsibility for your own actions and being able to live with the consequences. It teaches self- control and tolerance, empathy and understanding. It most certainly is not all about light hearted camaraderie and fun.

There is a very dark aspect to the Craft, as in all walks of life. Such knowledge is not offered or taught routinely as any part of the initiation process, but is sometimes available much later in our studies. Due to the nature of such teachings, the mentor must be one hundred per cent certain the student will be able to handle such knowledge and only ever with correct intent.

The only reason it should ever be taught is as a form of defence or protection. It is much easier to deal with negativity and darkness when you know how to recognise and repel it. This is where my earlier reference to Pandora's box comes in. Some people just cannot resist 'dabbling' in forbidden fruits and Witchcraft is no exception. For some, knowledge is power and with power often comes greed, a formidable mix, treacherous and sometimes downright dangerous.

This recipe for disaster is unfortunately not only confined to magic, it is in abundance throughout society and presents itself in many forms. Weak characters become seduced by misplaced feelings of their own grandeur and capabilities and become lost. When this happens they often choose to feed the fear in others seeing it as a source of power.

Craft Law does not tolerate such behaviour from amongst its own and perpetrators are dealt with swiftly and cast out for all time.

One of the Laws we live by, the Threefold Law, teaches us the concept of receiving back anything we give out, three times over. Simply put, this means that when you do something nice or good or kind for someone and your intentions are pure and from the heart, your actions will be repaid to you three times over in a good and positive way.

Equally, we must accept that if we do something bad or evil, this will also return to us three times over. Believe you me, this is exactly what happens and you really would not wish to be on the receiving end of such a powerful negative force. The Threefold Law, a law I believe we would all do well to live by, Witch or not.

Toward the end of the first year of study we are given a brief glimpse a 'Taster' if you like, of what is involved should we decide to continue with our studies to Second Degree. For a variety of reasons many go no further than First Degree and that is fine, but I had already made up my mind I wanted to continue and was eager to start the next part of my journey.

I was under no illusion that Second Degree would be very different to First Degree and it was, but in all honesty, I had no idea just how different that would be. It is most certainly not for the faint hearted.

I remember well the evening at Molly's, when I was asked if I wished to go ahead with Initiation to the First Degree. I tried to be calm and collect with my answer, I so wanted to appear aloof and nonchalant. That failed. I bumbled and blithered and in the end just could not hold it together any longer. I leapt up from my chair and ran across the room to Molly. I hugged and squeezed her so tight in my excitement I forgot the cat was on her lap. The cat meowed, Molly laughed so much she coughed uncontrollably and all three of us nearly fell out of her chair.

"I thought you might be pleased", said Molly, "good job I bought us all a cream cake to celebrate". The cat meowed again.

"OK, you can have some too", she said.

While Claire and I were busy devouring a slice or two of the scrumptious cake, Molly left the room for a while. She returned looking very pleased with herself.

"Well that's that then", she announced triumphantly, "the date is set. Your initiation will take place at Beltane camp".

"But that's only ……" I interjected.

"Yes, I know", Molly replied, "that's only three weeks away. You're going to be very busy, then aren't you? Well that should keep you out of mischief for a while and give us all a bit of peace and quiet for a change".

Molly and Claire looked at each other and giggled raucously.

The venue chosen for my initiation was kept secret from me, but I was told the ceremony would be closed. This meant only those of Second Degree and above would be **invited to** attend. Molly was to take care of all the arrangements, all I had to do was trust that all would be well.

The weeks before my initiation were very busy indeed. Many people were involved in the arrangements although I knew very little about what was going on. For my part I had to prepare myself physically, mentally and emotionally and spent much of my time meditating, reading, practising my lines and making my initiation gown.

White is the traditional colour of the first degree and therefore, following tradition, I chose to make a white gown embellished with silver thread, tiny crystals and silver sequins. It made me realise how much like a wedding an initiation really was. Both unions require many of the same qualities such as commitment, loyalty, trust, patience and understanding. It felt like I was 'marrying' the Craft and in a way, I suppose that's exactly what I was about to do.

As the day of initiation crept closer my excitement grew as did the number of questions I had going around and round in my head:

Who would be there, where was the venue, what would happen if I messed up my lines or gave the wrong answers, would that mean I had failed and couldn't be a First-Degree Witch, who was going to perform the ceremony and why had they chosen to 'close' it? Questions, questions so many questions.

I knew that choosing to close the initiation was an unusual step to take because First Degree is usually an open ceremony in recognition of the celebration that it is. No magic is performed during the initiation so there is no reason for it to be any other way.

Even so, I can honestly say not once did I question the decision or have any concerns or fears. I was about to move deeper into the bosom of my Witch family and I did so willingly and without doubt.

The days leading up to Beltane seemed to fly by and before we knew it my husband Michael and I were busy packing ready for camp.

We arrived at the chosen site just before mid-day amid the hectic scene of people trying to park their vehicles, put up tents and control uncontrollable children. There was much laughter and lots of hugging going on as friends met up again and in the centre of the field was the familiar site of the camp fire.

The fire at a Pagan gathering is usually one of the first things to be organised as it becomes the hub of the whole camp experience. It is the place where people arrange to meet, where you can cook if you want to and where everyone migrates to especially at night for company and entertainment. Our gatherings are never short of talented people who delight in providing us with music, dance, story-telling and singing. It is a place of comfort, communication, caring and sharing.

My husband Michael and I eventually found ourselves a place to park and began setting up camp under the shade of a magnificent oak tree. I was busy inside the tent getting things organised when there was a 'knock' on the canvas roof. I opened the flap at the entrance to the tent and found nothing, but a note flapping in the breeze tied to a guide rope. The message inside the note was to let me know Molly would be arriving at noon the following day and my initiation ceremony would take place at 3.00pm.

I was surprisingly calm about the whole thing and spent the rest of the day enjoying all the camp had to offer and catching up with old friends. Tomorrow was going to be a big day for me and wishing to keep a clear head so that I could savour every moment, as the evening began to draw in I said my good night's and retired to bed quite early.

I slept well and awoke the next morning just after dawn. Rubbing my eyes sleepily, I peeped out of the tent to find the only other creatures stirring were one or two dogs, a couple of children and the birds. I looked back at my husband still fast asleep snuggled up tight in his sleeping bag and smiled as he lay there snoring musically to himself. Very carefully, so as not to disturb him I managed to get dressed and slip quietly from the tent.

I made my way across the field and up the lane delighting in the treasures set before me. Early morning skies lit with a gentle corn yellow glow and just the faintest impression of a mist still hanging suspended in mid- air. I felt the cool kiss of dew upon my bare feet, a refreshing guilty pleasure. All around me the landscape sparkled, winking and glinting as though sprinkled with diamond dust. This world; our world; such beauty; such perfection.

Deep in thought I was busy collecting wild flowers ready to weave into my head dress when I came across an elderly lady sat on the step of a wooden style. I went over to speak with her and we ended up chatting for quite a while. She was an interesting lady with an air of enchantment about her.

She was old and yet young, wise and yet naïve. Deep lines etched into her face, each one a tale to tell and yet her beautiful green eyes shone radiantly with youthfulness. Wisps of silver grey hair framed her face, but still held the hint of what was once a fiery red mane.

Her jovial manner and obvious wit made our conversation flow easily and we were soon chatting as if we had known each other for ages. Such endearing qualities and such beauty all wrapped up in one tiny little parcel of a person. In her younger days, there was no doubt, she had been a temptress.

During our conversation, she told me she lived in an old barn further up the lane and had been there all her life. She mentioned that she rarely came out these days as her legs weren't too good, but today was a special day for her and anyway, who could resist being out and about on such a beautiful morning, she asked. I had to agree with her and on that happy note, we bid each other farewell and I made my way back to camp. With my mind full of the day ahead, I thought no more about her.

The rest of the morning flew by in a flurry of preparations for the ceremony. Before I knew it mid-day was upon us and I waited anxiously for Molly's arrival. I must admit the old nerves were beginning to kick in now, it wasn't that I was worried about anything it was more a mixture of excitement and raw emotion. I had worked so hard for this day and waited for what seemed to be an eternity and yet here we were it was happening – today, right here and right now.

I was in my tent pretending to be waiting patiently when a stranger appeared in the doorway. Without so much as a single word I was handed a piece of paper, it was a hand-written note asking me to remain in my tent until further notice.

I asked the stranger if Molly was here yet and could I see her please, but the stranger gave no reply he simply turned around and walked away. Oh great, I thought to myself, the silent treatment, oh well, better just get on with it then. I waited as instructed growing more impatient and more nervous with every passing moment. I really did want to see Molly I wanted to know if I looked alright, to practice my lines with her, ask some more questions. We had journeyed so far together, where was she?

Instead, my poor husband who was doing his best to keep me calm had to put up with the barrage of nervous rantings and chatter. He said all the right things as he always does and kept me calm like only he knows how.

It was during an endless stream of questions and the need for constant reassurance that we suddenly became aware of a deep throbbing sound far off in the distance. I so wanted to take just the tiniest sneaky peek to see what was going on, but I knew now was not the time to disobey a request. I stayed where I was listening to the hypnotic beat of the drums as they grew louder, they were getting closer. Suddenly, the flap of our tent drew back making us both jump and there, stood right in front of us was the tall lean figure of a man.

He wore a beautiful velvet cloak in shades of green and copper that fell heavily from his shoulders to the ground. His face was concealed with an intricately woven mask of leaves and lichen and upon his head there was a magnificent crown of antlers.

No one had told me this was going to happen and I didn't know whether to turn on my heels and exit through the back of the tent or stay put and go with the flow. I decided to stay where I was and see what happened next.

The man spoke with a voice as soft as his cloak. He asked me to state my name and the purpose of the ceremony I was about to take part in. I answered his questions rather hastily then promptly enquired if he knew where Molly was as I didn't want anything to start without her. He smiled reassuringly, but left my question unanswered, instead he told me to follow him in silence. I glanced back at my husband looking for his reassurance once more and pulled a face I make when I'm nervous. He smiled back at me, our eyes met and I knew everything would be alright, so I turned and stepped out of the tent.

I shall never forget the most wonderful and completely unexpected sight that stood before me. A huge crowd of people had gathered outside our tent every one of them in Beltane costume. I stopped for a moment to scan the beautiful palette of vibrant Spring colours, how lucky was I to have so many people wishing to share this special day with me, whoever they all were.

The drumming had dropped to a gentle crescendo, but as the procession left the field heading out along the lane, the volume rose once more stirring the atmosphere with excitement and anticipation.

We were led to a public footpath and after following its route for a short while, we veered off to the left heading deeper and deeper into the darkness of a pine forest. Each step we took sunk us further down into a deep spongy carpet of pine needles as our nostrils filled with the thick sweet scent of the forest.

We continued our journey through cathedral like spires of pine trees their trunks towering above us, until eventually the density and darkness of the forest gave way to a hidden treasure.

It was a woodland glade lit only by piercing shards of golden sunlight the whole area appearing to hover like some secret island floating on a sea of bluebells. I stopped to revel in the fragrance of the flowers and as I looked up I noticed people entering the glade were beginning to form a circle. I felt butterflies in my belly.

Suddenly the drumming stopped, the chattering crowd fell silent and an eerie stillness befell the place, no one moved. I had been called to a halt some way back from the perimeter of the glade and had been watching from a distance. Someone approached me from behind and just as I was about to turn around to see who it was, a man's voice bid me be still.

A blindfold was placed over my eyes, my arms were gently, but firmly taken round my back and my wrists were bound together. Two strong hands rested upon my shoulders and I was guided to walk forward.

My feet faltered at each step unsure of the ground beneath them. The haunting notes of a flute begin to play its tune and as the melody floated through the air I too, felt as though I were being lifted to glide effortlessly along the way.

And then I tripped, stumbling forward as I did so, a sharp scratch scoring itself across my left upper arm. I did not make a fuss, nor did I pass any comment, I simply carried on until the music stopped and I was told to stop. Once again there was silence. I had no idea where I Was being taken to, but I did know we had travelled way past the glade and I wondered how far away the others were.

The arms that had been guiding me dropped from my shoulders, I heard the snap and crack of twigs as they broke underfoot and I knew my guide was leaving me.

It seemed like I had been left on my own for a very long time so to pass the time and calm my nerves a little, I began to count how many different types of birdsong I could hear. Deeply immersed in the distraction I set myself, I became totally unaware of my surroundings and had not heard approaching footsteps. I was brought back to the here and now by a familiar voice that near on made me jump clear out of my skin. Very clearly and very purposefully the voice asked:

"Before this ceremony can begin I must ask of you this one question. How do you enter this Circle?"

"I enter this circle of my own free will in Perfect Trust and Perfect Love", I replied.

The ritual had begun.

\*\*\*

Out of respect for my fellow Brothers and Sisters of the Craft and its traditions the remainder of the ceremony stays between those who know and those who were there. I can tell you however, Molly had been there all the time, just as she had been every step of the way for the past thirteen Moons and more. She hadn't missed a single moment.

After the ritual I was carried back to camp upon a throne of white flowers. The procession marched through the campsite gathering well- wishers as we travelled and I felt like a Queen. On arrival at the camp fire I was lowered gently to the ground and as I stepped down from my throne a huge roar from the crowd rang out and the music and dancing began. The whole area was festooned with white balloons and bunting and garlands hung from every branch of nearby trees. The celebrations had begun and there was cakes and ale for all. We partied in style, something pagans seem to do very well and I knew the festivities would go on long in to the night. I stayed as long as I could, but eventually, exhausted from the day's events I returned to my tent for some peace and quiet and to reflect upon all that had happened.

The night air in May can be a tad chilly and I was busy struggling to pull on my jumper over my pyjamas when Molly appeared and asked if she could come in. We greeted each other affectionately, but in that single moment I sensed a sadness about her. I stepped back to look at her.

"Well, littl'un" she said, "you did me proud today as I knew you would and that is why I asked them to come".

"Who did you ask to come Molly?" I asked, rather puzzled by her statement.

Molly continued.

"Throughout our time together you have asked for nothing and questioned even less and now I have something to tell you. There are two very special people here that I would like you to meet".

She stood back and behind her were the High Priest and High Priestess who had initiated me. To protect their identity, I will refer to them as Simon and Katrina. They were no longer in ceremonial dress and I was secretly bemused to see how 'normal' they looked in 'civvies'. They were wearing jeans and t-shirts like everyone else at camp and blended in very well.

At their request, we left my tent and went to a quiet corner of the field where no one could disturb us and our conversation would not be overheard. We sat together on the grass and Molly began by explaining who Simon and Katrina really were. It turned out they were in fact a very well respected and well known married couple from the pagan community who belonged to one of the oldest pagan cultures of the British Isles.

I remember it was at this point I had an over whelming urge to courtesy or something, but I didn't, I stayed unusually still and quiet wanting to know more. They had travelled all the way from 'Middle England' as I shall refer to it, at Molly's request and had been receiving regular reports from her since day one of my training. The more I learnt about this couple the more I realised what a great honour it was they had come all this way just for me. What I couldn't work out was - why?

"Now you know who they are", said Molly, "I expect you would like to know exactly why they have travelled all this way?". She read my mind, she was always doing that. I was lost for words and just nodded.

"My, my, a rare event indeed" she went on, "what's the matter, cat got your tongue?" I nodded again.

"Goodness, I think she's star struck", Molly continued.

"Oh no, please don't ever feel like that about us", said Katrina kindly. She turned toward me and with a great big smile came over and gave me the biggest hug.

"After all, it is we who have been waiting such a long time to meet you, the honour is all ours".

"Really", I said in utter bewilderment.

"Oh yes, continued Katrina, since that very first night Molly rang us after meeting you at a local moot".

"But that was well over a year ago,", I said.

"Indeed! It was and Molly has kept us updated on your progress ever since".

To say by now I was totally flabbergasted would be a monumental understatement. I could not believe what I was hearing. Molly had not uttered a single word about this to me, not once. All this time and I had no idea what had been going on.

"The reason we have all been keeping such a close eye on you", said Simon, "is because Molly knew there was something extra-ordinary about you the moment she met you and it would appear as always, she was right". He smiled at Molly affectionately.

"We have a confession to make", said Katrina, "we did indeed come all this way to perform your initiation, but there is another reason we are here. We have a question to ask of you, a very important one and you will need time to think about things before you give your answer. We will give you all the time you need and please understand there is absolutely no pressure, whatever you decide we will respect your wishes".

I remember at this point thinking they had got me confused with someone else, why all the secrecy and who on earth did they think I was? This had to be a case of mistaken identity, either that or I had got over excited about my initiation and this was all a dream.

I couldn't imagine what the question was going to be so I kept quiet and waited for them to continue.

"As Molly, has explained", said Katrina, "Simon and I are from a very old Craft family and although much of what we do is very open, there is much that is kept completely closed. We belong to an 'Inner Circle' that is spoken of by no one outside of it. There is a reason for this. Those who believe the Burning times are over are fools. They will never be over and we have to be very careful in order to protect our way of life, our values, our traditions and each other".

Katrina was a gentle soul, I could tell and yet right now she spoke in a manner that was both serious and fiercely protective. She turned to Simon for him to continue.

"We have come all this way to personally invite you to join our Inner Circle. You will continue your studies under our direct supervision and answer to no one else. You will be free to mingle at local moots and events as you have always done, but your time with Molly will be finished. If you decide to join us you can tell no one and there are no exceptions, you will be sworn to absolute secrecy. This is not a game and we have a very strict code of conduct. Those who break our rules are not looked upon favourably and there will be consequences".

Simon's speech was from the heart and had been spoken with much pride and passion and despite the severity of his words I knew no threat had been intended. I was already aware for the need to protect such Circles. I had been part of one for a very long time.

"We have a long journey in front of us and will be leaving shortly", said Katrina, "have you any questions before we go?"

"Two things", I said, having finally found my voice. "Firstly, thank you from the very top and bottom of my heart for what you have done for me today and for making my First Degree so very special. Secondly, why me, who exactly do you think I am?"

"Two things", said Katrina with a cheeky grin on her face, "firstly you are very welcome it has been our pleasure and secondly, it is not a matter of who we think you are, more a case of who we know you are".

\*\*\*

Not long after we started working together, Claire found out she was expecting a baby and by Beltane she would be heavily pregnant. We had always planned to take our First Degree together, but all things considered, Claire decided to postpone her initiation until after the baby was born. Throughout her pregnancy, Claire continued her studies with me and Molly and was by my side throughout the Beltane celebrations. She even managed to waddle her way through my initiation ceremony and took great delight in teasing me about it because it meant she knew exactly what to expect at her initiation. Or so she thought!

The weeks after my initiation were relatively quiet and I was pleased of the lull, I had a lot of thinking to do and needed some time and space to myself. It was not a question of whether I wanted to join Simon and Katrina I knew the answer to that one before Simon had finished speaking. It was more to do with the obvious level of expectation they appeared to have of me and I genuinely had no idea why.

I rang Molly and asked if I could see her, maybe she would be able to throw a little more light on the subject. She seemed very pleased to hear from me and we arranged to meet the very next day.

I explained to her what was troubling me, but she already knew.

"That's a trait of yours I find truly endearing", she replied, "you really have no idea, do you?" I shook my head in agreement eager for her to continue.

"Well then", Molly chuckled, "if you are sitting comfortably, I shall begin".

Never in a million years could I ever have imagined what I was about to be told.

"You, my dear are the grand-daughter of Catherine Ivy, High Priestess and Witch Queen of one of the oldest surviving covens in the country. Catherine loved you from the moment she first clapped eyes on you".

"Her daughter, your mother, had never shown any interest in the Craft and this was a great disappointment to Catherine Ivy, but when you were born she knew things would be different".

Molly went on to explain the whole story.

My mother had gone into labour unexpectedly five weeks early and was alone in her caravan, where she and dad were living at the time. Realising something was wrong, she headed off across the field toward the end of the lane hoping to meet a passer-by who could raise the alarm. When someone finally did come past she explained what was happening gave them Nan's address and asked them to fetch her as quickly as they could. The message was never passed to Nan, but mum, thinking help was on its way decided to head back to the comfort of her caravan.

I, on the other hand decided I had waited long enough to enter this world and it was time to be born. Poor mum, she didn't make it back to the caravan.

Molly continued;

"In the meantime, your father had returned home from work to find the caravan door left open and no one at home. He could see the place had been left in a hurried state and sensing all was not well, set off across the field looking for your mother. Thank goodness, he did because he found you both barely alive in the middle of the field. Your mother was unconscious and had lost a lot of blood and there beside her, still and cold, was you".

The story continued, "Catherine Ivy had awakened that day with an uneasy sense of foreboding upon her so instead of going into town to meet with her sister as planned she decided to stay at home. She was busy in her kitchen kneading dough for the loaf of bread she was making when a vision of your mother came through and her blood ran cold. She knew instinctively something was wrong and your mother was in trouble. Without even wiping the dough from her hands she ran outside grabbed her bicycle and cycled as fast as she could toward the caravan".

"She arrived to find your father on his knees in the middle of the field cradling you and your mother in his arms sobbing uncontrollably. Catherine Ivy swung into action immediately and took control of the situation. She sent your father into the village to summon help whilst she attended to you and your mother".

"Having made sure your mother was breathing and in a comfortable position she turned her attention to you. Lifting you toward her face she covered your nose and mouth with her mouth and gently breathed life into your tiny lungs.

There was a sudden intake of breath a cough and a splutter, you let out an almighty shriek then opened your eyes. Your tiny little hands reached out to grasp one of Catherine's fingers and there they stayed as if clinging on to dear life itself".

"It was during that moment she saw the mark and knew it would be you who carried on in her footsteps. From those first, few precious moments a very strong bond was formed between the two of you, a bond that will never be broken".

All this while I had sat in stunned silence listening intently to what Molly had to say. I glanced down at my hand and the mark she was referring to, I said nothing. Molly continued.

"The mark is known as a bread mark, it's an old-fashioned term used to describe a birth mark. The one you bear is very distinctive because it only appears when exposed to the sun and only certain members of your family carry this mark".

She went on to describe the shape and position of the mark in detail and told me of the other members of my family who bore the same mark. She was right on all counts and I wondered how she seemed to know so much about us all.

I could not speak. I felt as if I was being battered by some raging sea as emotion after emotion swept over me. I wanted to cry, laugh, jump up and down, shout, scream. I didn't know what I wanted to do. What does one do when they hear such revelations? If only I had known all of this when Nan was alive we could have shared so much more, I could have worked with her in Circle.

Questions, questions and even more questions and why oh, why hadn't she shared her secret with me? It was to be some time later before the penny finally dropped and I realised that was exactly what she had been doing from the day I was born. The answers were all around me, I just hadn't learned how to find them yet.

Molly must have seen how upset and confused I was because rather abruptly she suggested we call it a day and continue our conversation another time.

I made my way home in a complete daze and only came back to the 'here and now' as my car bumped its way up on to the driveway of my cottage. I didn't go indoors straight away, instead I chose the solace of my beloved garden. I just couldn't take it all in, it was too much to fathom. I couldn't settle so I went for a walk wandering aimlessly about the village.

Cheerful greetings from passers-by appeared to me an unwelcome distraction from my private thoughts. Begrudging the intrusion, I turned around and headed back home.

Needless to say, I didn't get much sleep that night nor for several nights after that, but time ticked on as it does and gradually I began to feel calmer and more settled. I concluded I just had to accept what I had been told and carry on as usual, what else could I do?

One thing I did know for certain, I needed to share all this news with someone and there was only one person that could possibly be, Claire. We met and I told her everything that had happened.

"Well then", she said decisively, "you need answers and there's only one way we're going to get them now. We've got a ritual to do this week so let's ask the Goddess and see what She has to say".

So we did.

The night in question was a perfect night for working Magic. The Moon was Full and brilliant, shadows cast were long and dark and night time silhouettes looked as though they had been etched from an indigo palette.

Having cast a Circle of protection around us we prepared ourselves mentally then began our journey into the realms of the 'Other' worlds.

It all started on the banks of a beautiful lake where we found a boat tethered to some rocks by a length of frayed old rope. The rope hung against the sides of the vessel like draped curtains and as we climbed in to the boat, the rope slipped free from its guard filling the air with the musty smell of old twine.

The boat began to glide its way gracefully across the lake, peaceful silence broken only by the sound of water peeling lazily away from its bow. We were about half way across the lake when the boat came to an abrupt halt. Claire and I looked around us, but nothing appeared to be happening so we sat together quietly watching the Moon's reflection shimmer hypnotically upon the surface of the water.

It was a still night, there was no wind, no breeze not even a whisper so imagine our surprise when all of a sudden the surface of the water began to quiver and ripple. Slowly, but surely the glistening reflection of the plump round Moon began to change shape forming the outline of a person's face. I recognised it immediately.

Without even thinking I stood up clambering carelessly to the other side of the boat making it rock mercilessly from side to side. Claire reached out to grab the back of my jacket just as we were flung backward landing in a heap between the wooden seats.

I sobbed uncontrollably to the point where I could not speak. Claire put her arm around my shoulders to comfort me as we stared intently upon the face that had formed before us. It was Nan.

I was afraid if I took my eyes of the reflection for even one second it would disappear and she would be gone again. I need not have worried, the face in the water remained and then it spoke to us.

'My darling girl, the fact that you are here tells me you are travelling the path of the Old Ones, just as I always hoped you would. I know you have many questions, but you must be patient, the answers you seek will come in time.

So, now you know who I am and more importantly, who you are. I am sorry I could not tell you myself, I had to be sure this time. You see I made a terrible mistake with your mother, I took it for granted she would naturally follow in my footsteps, but she did not. I did little to hide my disappointment and that was wrong of me.

It was her decision and her choice to make, but for a long time this caused trouble between us and I deeply regret that. We spent many precious years apart because of this, such a waste. I did not want to make the same mistake with you and decided right from the outset that this time, I would let fate take its course.

If the Craft was to become your way of life too, then you must find your own way and make your own choices. And here you are. I am so very proud of you. Travel the path well, travel it wisely, keep love in your heart always and know that whenever you think of me, I am already there".

The water rippled and she was gone.

My eyes were stinging with tears, my throat was tight with grief and yet in those few short moments so many things began to fall into place. I missed her so much.

Signalling the end of this encounter the boat began to turn around and headed back toward the shoreline. We arrived at the shallow waters edge, climbed out of the boat and returned to the here and now.

"That's enough for tonight", said Claire, "let's close down and go inside".

We went indoors and wrote about the night's events in our book of shadows.

"Know something?" asked Claire, as we sat scribbling away in our books, "there was a moment back there whilst we were at the lake, when I half expected to see a sword rise up out of the water". We both giggled at the thought - as if.

A few days later I went to see Molly to tell her what happened. She confirmed the relationship between Nan and my mother had been a very difficult one and their issues with each other had never truly been resolved. When I came along Nan was determined not to make the same mistake again, if I was to follow in her footsteps I would have to find my own way **there**. Therefore, she had gone to such extra-ordinary lengths to make sure that was exactly what happened.

Molly went on to tell me much more about my grandmother's life as a Witch Queen. The more I learned, the more I filled with pride, if only I had known.

Eventually Molly put her hand up in the air and said it was time to stop for today. I had already pleaded with her several times not to stop, to tell me one more thing, but I could see she was getting tired so reluctantly we drew the meeting to a close.

"Before you go", she said, "I have something for you, wait there one moment" and she shuffled off into another room On her return, she was carrying something wrapped in layers of linen and cotton cloth. She set the item down on the dining room table with a thud, whatever it was, it was certainly heavy.

She moved around the table slowly un-wrapping the bundle peeling away the layers of cloth one at a time. When at last she finally stepped back holding the article high in front of her, I nearly fell over in disbelief.

She was holding a sword.

"I present to you with great pride and with the greatest of Honour, 'Gwyddion', now placed in your charge".

Again, I was speechless, all I could think of was those last few words Claire had spoken the other night about the sword rising from the lake, and here it was. Wait till Claire sees this, I thought to myself.

Gwyddion is beautiful and almost as big as me. He is made from hand forged steel with a brass hilt encrusted with semi-precious stones. The handle is bound in hand-hammered leather and the shaft is exquisitely inscribed with magical symbols in the ancient hand of the Picts. A true treasure indeed and now it was being entrusted to me.

"Only ever to be used in ceremonial magic, you know this of course" confirmed Molly as I took hold of it and nearly buckled under its weight. I nodded in acceptance of her words.

"When you have found out what all the symbols and inscriptions mean you are ready to use it. When the time is right, you too will pass it on. This is our way, now and for all times as it has been for centuries".

I began to thank Molly, but she interrupted me and said:

"There is no need for any thanks my dear, it is yours by right. I've just been looking after it for you. It was your Grandmother's. Now you are its Keeper and all is as it should be, once more".

Claire came over the next day and listened intently as I told her all about my meeting with Molly. By the end of the account she was practically falling off her stool with excitement.

"Please go and get the sword", she said, "I can't wait a moment longer to see it".

I left the room to fetch Gwyddion and on my return, was so wrapped up in presenting the sword as dramatically as I could I hadn't noticed Claire turning paler by the second. She raised an arm pointing a finger at the sword and I noticed she was visibly trembling.

"That's it, that's it", she kept saying.

"What's 'it'?", I asked growing increasingly concerned about her well- being whilst trying to sit her down before she fell.

"That's the sword I used to draw right from a small child, everywhere, all over my school books, everywhere. Turn it over I want to see the writing, the strange writing on the back, I know it's there, it has to be".

I turned it over to show her the writing as requested.

"I feel sick", she said and promptly fainted.

Four and a half hours later Claire gave birth to a beautiful baby girl and named her Lily. It was all so fast I still can't believe the chain of events that took place, neither of us can. As Claire fainted her waters broke, I called an ambulance, the ambulance got caught in traffic, a neighbour heard the commotion and came around to see if she could help, she was a midwife and Lily was born on my kitchen floor!

Later that evening I was sat on Claire's bed in the local cottage hospital holding Lily. How quickly everything had changed. Claire was sleeping. She awoke with a start, sat bolt upright in her bed, looked at me and said; "Promise me one thing, next time you get Gwyddion out, make sure I'm not nine months pregnant" and we both fell about laughing.

Claire and Lily were soon home and settling in well to their new life as mother and daughter. I left them alone for a while to get used to being a family until one afternoon, Claire telephoned asking me to go over and visit.

"I have something to show you", she said, "bring Gwyddion with you, I promise I won't faint".

I arrived at Claire's and was amazed at how quiet it was.

"Lily is sleeping", said Claire, "let's make the most of it, she won't be quiet for long".

We took a cup of tea out into the garden and sat under the cool shade of the apple tree. On the table were pieces of paper and old school books filled with sketches and doodles. They looked as if they had been done by a child and I told Claire this.

"They were", she said, "I was the child".

On closer inspection, I could see the paper was well worn and some of the drawings had faded slightly. The notebooks were a familiar site to me they were the typical school exercise book with pale grey lines and a pink line down one side for the margin. They even smelt like school and for a moment I was transported back to memories of my classroom days.

Some of the patterns Claire had drawn I did not recognise, but some of them I did. A few of the inscriptions had been grouped together and words written underneath in modern day English.

"But this is what's..." I began to say.

"Yes, I know", she proclaimed triumphantly, "this is what is written on 'G' and what is even spookier, I remember watching and helping someone do the inscribing".

"Memories of a previous life time", I asked quizzically.

Claire shrugged her shoulders.

We looked at each other, then at 'G', the name we now used affectionately when referring to the sword, we looked again at the sketches and writings. Too stunned to speak, we sat side by side in silence trying to work out just exactly what was going on here.

"Well, I guess there's only one thing left to do then", I said, "let's find out what all these inscriptions mean. It's time for 'G' to tell his story".

Over the next few weeks we met as often as we could to find out as much as we could about the mystery sword.

Mr 'Google' went into overdrive we used the internet so much, we visited book shops, went to lots of pagan meetings and events, spent hours sat amongst mountains of dusty old books until eventually, bit by bit the pieces of the puzzle came together and 'G' began to reveal his secrets.

Feeling rather chuffed with ourselves and everything we had managed to find out, we figured it was time to pay Molly a visit so that she could confirm our findings. After all, we wouldn't want to be turning people into toads instead of frogs now, would we?

I rang Molly's telephone number several times, but each time there was no answer. I knew she didn't go out much so one afternoon on the spur of the moment Claire and I decided to drive over to see her.

We pulled in to the close where Molly lived to find a removal van outside her house. At first, we didn't take too much notice, I suppose we both took it for granted it was a neighbour that was moving so we carried on and parked the car.

Having finally got Lily and all her paraphernalia sorted out, Claire went on ahead of me proudly pushing the pram toward Molly's front gate. I was busy trying to shove 'G' into my sports bag in the hope it may save me having to explain what I was doing in the middle of the day lugging a sword the same size as me, into an old lady's house, when suddenly I went cold.

I turned around to see Claire talking with one of the removal men then gasp out loud clasping her hand to her mouth. I dropped everything and ran as fast as I could toward them, I couldn't imagine what had invoked such a reaction from Claire.

I arrived just in time to hear Claire ask the man;

"How long did you say?" and I noticed she was gripping the handle bar of the pram so tight her knuckles had gone white. The man continued:

"Seven years now this place been empty. No one from round 'ere would come near it, council's well 'appy someone's finally moving in. The new folk aren't from round 'ere see, so they don't know the story".

"Story, what story would that be then?" I asked, not really knowing if I truly wanted to find out.

"A right odd one if you ask me", said the man.

"See, there was this old dear lived 'ere, some say she was a Witch. Got up to all sorts of strange things by all accounts. Became frail and couldn't manage on her own anymore.

Council wanted 'er out, place was beginning to fall into disrepair. Be best for 'er they said, if she went into one of them care home places.

People was afraid of 'er really I reckon. Problem was she didn't want to go, insisted she was stayin' cos she was waitin' for someone. Try as they might she would not budge until suddenly, one day not so very long ago, the neighbours woke up to find she'd gone. 'Er and that cat of 'ers, just vanished into thin air they did".

"Rumour 'as it, she went to live with 'er sister in the old barn up Jannings Lane, but that ain't right, it burnt down years ago."

With that, he turned away and carried on moving furniture into Molly's house, but it wasn't Molly's furniture and it wasn't Molly's house anymore.

To say we were stunned would be a gross understatement, but somehow Claire and I were beginning to get used to such things happening one way or another.

We got back into the car and decided to drive to Jannings Lane in search of Molly. I knew exactly where it was, it was the lane leading into the field we had camped in at Beltane. It was the same lane where I had met the old lady on the morning of my initiation. What if the old lady was in fact Molly's sister?

That being the case, both they and the barn were still there, the removal man must have been mistaken. I distinctly remembered the old lady telling me she lived in a barn further on up the lane so the plan was we would go and find her and ask if she knew our friend Molly.

We arrived in the lane soon enough parked the car and took a leisurely stroll along the pathway. It was a beautiful afternoon, the sun was shining, birds were singing and all was well with the world. Lily had fallen asleep and Claire and I were engrossed in a moment of pure botanical pleasure having stumbled across a cornucopia of native British herbs. They were quite rare ones to find these days like eyebright, white wild violets, agrimony and soapwort and yet here they were, growing in abundance throughout this magical hedgerow. We were so busy photographing our finds and discussing whether they were or weren't this herb or that, we hadn't noticed time flying by.

"Oh crumbs, look at the time", said Claire, "we'll have to start heading home soon, better get a wriggle on if we are going to find this barn today".

The lane seemed to be carry on for miles and miles and we were just about to turn around and make our way back to the car, when a tractor came trundling slowly and noisily towards us. It was a wide vehicle and as it moved closer toward us it became obvious there wasn't going to be enough room for all of us to pass safely.

Claire and I hastily clambered on to the bank of the ditch dragging the pram behind us. The heavily laden metal monster drew level alongside us and ground to a cough spluttering halt.

A ruddy red face poked its way out from the window of the tractor cab greeting us heartily.

"Afternoon me lovelies, don't often see people this far down the lane, especially pushing a pram. Sheep's we see, lots of them critters, but not often one of them things", said the owner of the face pointing to the pram.

The man in the tractor jumped down of the kickboard and came toward us.

"You can come down out of that ditch me dears, I ain't gonna eat you. Mrs done me a right good lunch she did, lucky for you I'm full up. You lost then?" he asked.

We explained what we were doing there and who we were looking for and at that point the jolly farmer became more serious. It was as if someone had flicked a switch.

"The old barns you say, two sisters eh, well I think you're a bit late me dears, by about fifty years or more I'd say. Barn burnt down a long time ago, took the sisters with it. Sad day that was, sad day, never found the bodies. Sad day".

With that the farmer hoisted himself back up into his tractor cab, gave a wave and carried on down the lane. Claire and I looked at each other, said nothing, turned around and went home. This was all getting too strange and way too far beyond a joke.

I spent that evening at Claire's house and once we had all eaten and Lily had gone to bed Claire and I set about trying to find out what had happened to Molly.

I was in the kitchen making us both a cup of tea and deep in thought began to stir the milk round in one of the cups, the metal spoon clinking and clanging noisily against the china. I jumped as Claire spoke, I hadn't heard her come into the kitchen. I shall never forget the look on her ashen face, it was the look of fear and total bewilderment.

"You need to stop that and come and look at this," she said.

I followed her into the lounge as she guided me toward the computer. She had been looking at an archive of local newspaper clippings. A page on the computer screen was open and I sat motionless as I read the report.

The report recorded the following:

Two twin sisters had lost their lives in a barn blaze in Jannings Lane. Their names were Amanda and Millicent, affectionately known to locals as Mandy and Molly. They had lived together their whole lives and were rarely seen apart.

On the afternoon of the blaze, Molly had gone into the village to do some shopping whilst Mandy stayed at home doing some baking.

Evidence gathered during the investigation suggested that Mandy had fallen asleep in her chair by the range and a tea towel had slipped from the airer above landing on one of the hot plates. It was believed that on her return from the village Molly found the place ablaze and had entered the barn in a vain attempt to save her sisters life. No bodies were ever found.

The entry was dated 1954, that was over sixty years ago, Claire and I hadn't even been born.

The Molly mystery remains to this day just that, a total mystery. I asked Simon and Katrina about Molly, their response to my questions were simple. They asked me if, by meeting this wonderful old lady had I learnt anything? The answer was of course a resounding great 'Yes'. They asked me if I believed I had met her, the answer was, 'No', I did not believe I had met her, I knew I had.

"Indeed, you did, said Katrina, Molly was as alive then as she ever was, all you have to do is remember that".
Conversation closed.

The remainder of my journey through the Degrees of the Craft continued to the dizzy heights of Third Degree and the title of High Priestess and Witch Queen. Over the years, I have taught many in the ways of 'The Old Ones' and am proud to say that every one of them went on to take their Third Degree. For that honour and privilege, I have earned the right to wear the Blue Garter. My charges have long since 'hived off' and many of them now have their own teaching circles and covens. I thank every one of them for all they have taught me in the process and wish them well.

I am of the Old school and do not feel it necessary to discuss or reveal our ceremonies and rituals. In any case, many others have already done that. It is my belief that some things should remain private and between those who 'know' and those who do not and I choose to honour that belief.

What I will share with you however are some of the amazing experiences I have had along the way as they are just too good to leave out. Like the time…

\*\*\*

# Norfolk

I will never forget the night I was tied to a tree stark naked in the middle of a forest in Norfolk!

True indeed, it was part of my second-degree initiation ceremony and Claire and I had been summoned to make the long journey from the South Coast all the way to the wind battered coasts of Norfolk.

We arrived at the train station after a gruelling six-hour journey tired, but excited. Only problem was, there was no one there to meet us and we hadn't a clue what we were supposed to do next. We had no contact telephone numbers to let them know we had arrived and no address to go to. All we had been given was the date of the ceremony and travel details to a station, where upon our arrival we were to await further instruction. With no one there to meet us we had no option, but to wait it out, be patient and Trust.

The weather was beginning to turn colder by the minute and in an effort to keep warm we paced up and down the platform restlessly. We waited and waited, but still no one came. The month was November and the darkness of night fell early. Claire and I had stopped talking to each other our lips too numb to form words, so we sat together on a wooden bench and huddled up close for warmth.

A strange feeling of eeriness began to creep over us as we started to fidget and squirm, glancing here, glancing there. Then out of the silence came a loud creaking noise and the large metal gate next to the ticket office laboured its way open.

The platform sign hanging above our heads began to swing furiously as a tall dark figure came toward us. Claire and I stood up as the figure drew near, their cloak billowing out behind them in the wind. The figure stopped about ten feet or so away from us head bent forward and covered with a hood. Not a word of greeting or introduction was uttered as an arm appeared from deep within the warmth of the cloak and a finger beckoned us to follow.

We were ushered toward a waiting car and as we approached the two side doors at the back of the car swung open. We clambered in without the slightest thought for our own safety, just grateful to be getting out of the cold, cold wind. As strange and as dramatic as this all might seem we knew we were in safe hands, whoever they belonged to.

The driver was dressed in the same sort of hooded robe as the person who had come to collect us, they too offered no greeting and did not reply to ours. We settled into our seat, the car engine started up and away we went. Needless to say, it was a very quiet journey, no one spoke, Claire and I because we couldn't and our chauffeurs because apparently, they didn't.

After about twenty minutes or so, we arrived at a bed and breakfast establishment right on the beach front at Cromer. The car pulled up at the bottom of a steep flight of steps, the doors of the car swung open and Claire and I got out.

Our luggage had been left in a heap on the pavement and whilst we were busy sorting it all out we hadn't noticed the car doors closing behind us. The engine started up again and the car was gone. Just like that. Having been deposited outside the guest house we concluded this was obviously where 'They' wanted us to be, so we gathered our belongings and turned toward the steps.

A bitter wind blew in from the sea, cruel and unyielding it carried sharp sand from the nearby beach that bit into our faces.

"Oh great", said Claire, "now we're gonna get shot blasted into the bargain".

"Never mind", I replied, "let's think of it as an exfoliating face mask", we both giggled.

I remember to this day, the absolute joy of feeling warm air blow over us as we entered the foyer of the guest house. There was no one about just a big brass bell shining brightly on the desk in reception beckoning to be rung.

"Crumbs, Faulty Towers or what?" said Claire as we admired the large majestic stairwell and the huge stained glass central window in the hallway.

It was the first time either of us had spoken since we left the station platform and it was nice to be back to some sort of normality. We rang the bell and the loudness of its ring made us both jump. Claire forgot there was a suitcase behind her and fell backward sliding down the arm of a huge leather chair till she landed upside down in its seat.

We laughed so much I couldn't do anything to help her at first. Eventually, I managed to pull myself together and went over to haul her out of the seat. As I leaned forward to pull her up she reached out grabbing my arm and pulled me into the chair with her. There we were, two grown adults upside down in a chair, laughing so much we couldn't breathe and totally oblivious to the man who had appeared behind the desk.

"Hrrrm, hrrrm", the man cleared his throat to get our attention. "This way please. Your room is ready, we've been expecting you".

Claire and I looked at each other then started laughing all over again as we tried to fight our way out of the chair and gather our belongings.

The room we were taken to was large, comfortably furnished and warm and after a good look round we decided it was time to unpack. We were busy getting ourselves organised when there came a knock at the door. The door opened and in came the man from reception with a tray of piping hot tea and fruit scones. I had forgotten how hungry I was.

"Oh yes", he said, as he was turning to leave, "I nearly forgot, I have a message for you. Please be ready and waiting in reception at 9.00pm this evening. Dinner has been booked for you downstairs in the restaurant for 7.00pm and your account here has already been settled".

With that, he left the room closing the door behind him.

"I bet his name's Basil" said Claire, chuckling to herself as we began to tuck into the scones and tea.

We arrived in the restaurant a little before 7.00pm as instructed and still rather full of scones. No surprise then to find that neither of us had much of an appetite, but not wanting to appear ungrateful we both ordered homemade soup and a crusty roll. It was actually rather good and normally the only thing left on our plates would be the pattern, but not tonight. Tonight, we had other things on our minds.

Having finished the meal, we politely made our excuses and returned to our room. It was time to get ready for the night ahead.

Claire's role during the proceedings was that of Maiden and as such, part of her duties included helping me to get ready. I wanted to go through my lines one last time so whilst I was busy doing that, Claire kindly ran me a bath.

The bath was one of those old-fashioned enamel ones complete with black cast iron claws for feet. It must weigh a ton I thought to myself as I listened to the echoing sound of water cascading into the huge tub.

My senses were awakened by the exquisite aroma of essential oils of rose and patchouli, their fragrance riding majestically upon the tiny droplets of steam wafting in from the bathroom. Rose to reflect unconditional love and patchouli for grounding and protection. A perfect choice I thought to myself, Claire had chosen well and I found myself nodding in silent approval.

Try as I might, I just could not concentrate any more, what I didn't know now I never would so I lay back amongst the luxuriously soft pillows on the bed and let my mind wander wherever it wanted to go. Which turned out to be not very far at all, as the next thing I knew I was being woken by the sound of Claire's voice.

"Come on sleepy head, you choose your moments don't you. Now is not the time to drift off into a deep sleep. Chip chop, the waters getting cold".

I grudgingly left my peaceful slumber and dragging myself off the bed headed into the bathroom behind Claire. A gasp of pure delight left my lips as I slowly began to take in the scene set before me.

The room had been lit entirely with tiny tea light candles dancing and flickering playfully as they gave off their warm amber glow. Crystals winked and flashed their luminous sparkles all around the room whilst music played quietly in the background.

It was like a faerie grotto, I let my bath robe slide to the floor and stepped slowly and delightfully into a sumptuous sea of tranquillity. Leaning back into the bath I felt my un-acknowledged tensions melt away as the water enveloped me like a comforting silky smooth blanket. Just for a moment I wallowed in the sheer luxury of total, uninhibited relaxation then 'Wham' and just a single thought slammed me back to reality. I felt sick to my stomach. Second Degree, oh my, this is it, the process had begun. I was about to take yet another deeper step into the world of the Witch. Yes, I was nervous as hell, but I couldn't wait.

Time flew by and before we knew it 9.00pm had arrived and it was time to make our way down to reception as instructed. 'Basil' was stood behind the desk and without even glancing up from the paper he was reading, he said,

"Your taxi's already here, waiting outside for you. Enjoy your evening" and I'm sure I saw the faintest trace of a smile upon his lips.

It wasn't a taxi we found outside waiting for us, it was the same car and the same driver that had picked us up from the station and it quickly became apparent he still hadn't discovered the art of conversation.

I was pleased of the peace and quiet to be honest, it gave me the opportunity to experience a myriad of emotions as they swept over me one by one, curiosity, excitement, a little fear maybe, anxiety definitely and perhaps even a hint of pride. This was such an important next step in the life of a witch and I knew it. I also had a feeling this night was going to be very special indeed, but I could never have imagined how.

We travelled only a few miles or so before the car veered off from the main road to follow a gravel track. The further we headed down the track, the darker our surroundings became as densely planted trees appeared to encircle us as we travelled.

The road was bumpy to say the least and I was beginning to wish I hadn't bothered with the soup when luckily the car came to an abrupt halt. The driver got out, came around to my side of the car opened the door and beckoned us to get out. He then got back into the car and drove off without so much as a by your leave.

\*\*\*

We tried to look around us to get our bearings, but the darkness of the night meant it was like looking for a piece of jet in a colliery. Here we were again, in the middle of nowhere without a clue as to what happens next and then we heard it, the gentle hum of a car engine way off in the distance. The sound got louder and louder until eventually we could make out headlights coming toward us. With a cough and a splutter the vehicle finally ground to a halt the doors swung open and out got two robed figures.

"Oh no, not cousin 'It' again", whispered Claire as they headed toward us. "So, you don't think much of my acting skills then?" said one of the robed figures as they pulled back the hood of their cloak.

Claire and I shrieked with joy, it was Simon and the other mysterious robed figure turned out to be Katrina. I have rarely been so pleased to see anyone.

After a few moments of hugging and excited greetings Simon asked if we were ready, if I was ready. We assured him we were and with that he assumed a more serious tone, turned away and led us deeper into the forest.

The only noise to be heard was the sound of our own footsteps as we followed in silence until eventually, we arrived at the most magical site I had ever seen. A forest glade lit with hundreds of tiny lamps and candles and as I looked around I realised we were inside a most perfect circle of trees. Magical, totally magical and I began to ponder how they ever got to find such places.

Set in the middle of this enchanting space was the altar beautifully decorated with flowers and glistening crystals and all around us the ground sparkled with fairy dust.

Simon came toward me.

"I will ask you once more", he said, "are you ready?"

"I am ready" I replied.

Simon raised his arms in the air and declared;

"Let the ceremony begin".

From the darkness of the night came a throbbing sound of drum beat and the circle of trees began to fill with people.

I was called to stand before the altar where I was duly blindfolded, stripped naked then led away and tied to a tree with cords. As the last knot was fastened I noticed the beat of the drums getting quieter and quieter and realised they were leaving this sacred space.

I listened intently until I could hear the drums and people no more. I called out in a somewhat feeble voice hoping maybe just one person had stayed to watch over me, but there was no reply. I had been left all alone in the middle of a forest, in the middle of the night, totally defenceless, naked and tied to a bloody tree!

Was this really a good idea I asked myself, did I really want this so much I was willing to put myself in danger like this?

The more I thought about the situation and my vulnerability the more nervous I became so I decided to help keep myself calm I would sing a song. I soon realised that perhaps this wasn't a good idea after all, firstly because I can't sing and secondly, because I certainly didn't want to draw attention to myself so the song such as it was, became an almost inaudible hum.

An owl hooted, a fox called and a pigeon took flight from a nearby hedge, my senses went into overdrive. Something very lightly, almost gossamer like brushed across my thigh then my cheekbone and I froze.

What the hell was that? Fear began to rise within me. Stay calm, stay calm, I told myself, this is only the beginning I knew I was being tested. I sang louder calling for my Goddess to protect me. I started to fidget against the rough bark of the tree in an effort to free myself of this obvious intrusion tearing the skin on my back as I did so. Blades of grass tickled my legs and feet and I was beginning to get cold.

Then came a loud 'Crack', the unmistakable sound of twigs breaking underfoot, but who's foot I wondered? 'Crack' again. Sheer terror now coursed through my body, I wanted to cry out for help and yet too afraid to utter even a peep, I stayed silent. My imagination was beginning to run riot, I could hardly breathe the fear was so great. Everything began to swirl around in my mind and I started to feel sick.

Pull yourself together I told myself, have faith and trust and know you will not be harmed. In, out, breathe easy, relax.

'Crack'.

"That's torn it," said a man's voice from nearby. "Don't be afraid, he called out, I'm here to watch over you and keep you safe, but you're not supposed to know I am here".

A feeling of instant panic swept over me quickly replaced by a sense of relief that I was not alone, I froze again. How did I know this man was genuine, what if he was here to do me harm  My mouth went dry and I started to shake, a lone tear trickled down my cheek. I was totally defenceless. I opened my mouth to cry out in hope the others would hear me and come hurrying back, but no sound came out. I could hear the man's footsteps clearly now, he was much closer, close enough to see I was afraid.

"Oh no, please don't cry", said the voice. You really have no need to be afraid. I am here to watch over you, I've been here all the time. I belong to the same group as Simon and Katrina and I know exactly what is going on here and why you are tied to a tree. I was there myself a few years back".

My thought processes were working at warp speed as he spoke digesting all the information I could retrieve about what he had just said. He obviously knew who had bought me here and didn't seem at all phased by the fact that he was talking to a naked lady who was tied to a tree in the middle of the forest in the middle of the night, like you do.

Another thing, how on earth would anyone find this place unless they already knew it existed? I quickly set him a test and asked:

"Who are you and how do you come to me?"

"I am a brother of the Craft and I come to you in Perfect Trust and Perfect Love" came the unfaltering reply.

I breathed a huge sigh of relief replaced immediately by an overwhelming wish I had started the diet I was on several weeks earlier.

Conversation between us came easily and I was deeply engrossed in a recollection of his about a past life time as a Celtic Warrior, when we heard the unmistakable sound of the others returning.

"Please don't tell them I let the side down and gave the game away" he said and as our laughter faded I knew he was already leaving me.

"No, wait, please don't go yet", I called out to him. "I don't even know your name, I want to thank you for looking out for me…….hello, hello, are you still here?"

From a distance came this reply:

"It has been my pleasure as always to watch over you and keep you safe. I've been doing it for centuries. As for my name, you already know it ……..it's Gwyddion".

# And Paddy came too

It was Winter Solstice and Michael and I had been busy preparing for celebrations to be held at our home later that evening. The house we lived in at the time had the most perfect secluded garden that was just right for performing our rituals and celebrations and the coven often worked here.

Apart from the usual two-legged variety of coven members our Circles were Blessed with the presence of some four legged members too, our beloved dogs. Everyone was well used to their antics which was just as well because the dogs absolutely insisted on joining in the festivities whatever the occasion or weather. The presence of animals in Circle is considered a Blessing and they were always very welcome.

Foxy-lady was a beautiful white German Shepherd and although she always joined us, she only ever sat outside of the working space with her paws just touching the edge of the Circle.

Paddy on the other hand, was our beautiful Collie and not only came right in to Circle, he insisted on sitting right in front of the altar and once settled there, he would not budge an inch.

Then there was Lunar, she was our tri-coloured German Shepherd who did exactly whatever she wanted to and was always involved one way or another. One of her favourite tricks was to herd us all in to Circle then sit and watch intently, making sure no one left until she decided they could.

The password for an uninterrupted exit was a bonio biscuit, a trick she had learnt from a very early age and to this day it remains a mystery who taught her this party piece.

This night, however, it was Paddy's turn to take centre stage.

Everyone had arrived and we were gathered outside in the garden waiting for the ceremony to begin. The night sky was as black as ink its darkness broken only by the twinkling of tiny stars glistening like diamonds.

The air was cold and crisp our breath appearing like tiny clouds before us as we chatted and then through the night air, came the low, bellowing tone of the Horn calling us to order. All conversation ceased, the procession fell into place and we began to make our way down to the dell at the bottom of the garden.

During Winter Solstice, we are celebrating the end of long dark winter nights and a time of quiet reflection, to be replaced with the vibrancy of the return of the Sun and its promise of longer, lighter days to come. Usually, part of the ceremony will involve two male members of the group taking part in a mock battle between the Holly King, representing Winter (The Dark) and the Oak King, representing Spring and Summer (The Light). At this time of the year it is the Holly King who is defeated as He bows to the strength of the Oak King who wins the battle and now reigns supreme. And so the Wheel turns.

As we approached the working area little squeals of pure delight could be heard from people as they discovered the scene set out before them.

It was like a fairy tale winter wonderland. The whole place had been beautifully decorated with boughs of holly, ivy and mistletoe. Handmade decorations such as ginger bread men, candy canes, cinnamon sticks and dried citrus fruits were tied with red ribbon and hung from the branches of nearby bushes. Lanterns hung from the trees, their flickering flame dancing upon tiny crystals of frost making them sparkle as if winking at us playfully.

This was going to be a memorable celebration, you could just feel it.

The ritual went well and we had reached the point of making the offering when it became only too clear, there wasn't one, it had completely disappeared.

Claire and I had spent the afternoon baking traditional ginger bread biscuits. Some we used for decorations, some were for the offering and the rest were to be enjoyed either at cakes and ale or to be taken home by guests as token gifts.

We hunted high and low, on the altar, under the altar, in the equipment trunk, behind the trunk, we looked everywhere.

OK, so who's hidden the gingerbread men?

These were no ordinary plain old brown gingerbread men, oh no, these were very special, festive fun gingerbread men and we had covered them with fluorescent red, green and gold edible sparkle.

After much merriment and playful hunting around the coven members concluded Claire and I had actually forgotten to bring them with us. No matter how hard we tried to convince everyone we had left the gingerbreads on the altar our pleas appeared to be falling on deaf ears, until from out of the crowd someone asked the question, where was Paddy this evening?

Good question I thought, where indeed was he, after all, we were usually tripping over him at the altar. We called him, whistled for him, opened Circle and checked up at the house, we looked in the garden shed, the garage, the green house, all over the place, but he was nowhere to be seen.

We gathered together and decided something was seriously amiss. Paddy never missed Circle, not once, so we closed the ceremony and prepared to go in search of him. The mood quickly changed from one of fun and laughter to a sombre silence as the fact began to hit home to us all, Paddy was missing.

How things can change in an instant.

At the beginning of the ceremony we piled our hats and coats on top of a wooden trunk like we usually do to keep them off the cold damp ground. We used the trunk to carry all the ritual gear in and apart from a coat stand, it sometimes served as a seat or even a table. The pile of hats and coats had formed quite a mound and as people began to remove their belongings from the top of the trunk one of the women let out a gasp clasping her hands firmly over her mouth.

Everyone rushed over to see what had startled her and as we peered over the edge of the trunk, there he was, Paddy, in all his glory alive and well, thank goodness.

Totally hidden from view he had obviously decided to ignore our frantic calls and whistles, he was far too busy. Far too busy that is munching his way through the gingerbread men. He continued to lay on his spot, front paws crossed over one another, delicately holding his latest victim and blatantly ignoring our enquiring gaze.

For a moment or two we just stood there staring at him until eventually, he looked up at us all, his nose covered in sparkling glitter, turned himself around to face away from his audience, laid back down again and carried on eating.

No one could contain themselves any longer and we all fell about laughing. What a hoot. Paddy was not impressed with our behaviour. He glanced back toward us with an unmistakable glare of pure indignation in his eyes, picked up what was left of the gingerbread man he was devouring and proceeded to remove himself to another more civilised part of the garden.

We laughed and laughed until tears ran streaming down our faces, no one could speak let alone try to call him back and then someone asked the question;

"I wonder if Paddy's poo will sparkle?" and that started us all off again.

It did, for days, but at least we didn't have any trouble finding it!

# The day the Fith-Fath moved

It was late one afternoon and I was deeply engrossed in trying to work out some needlework instructions when the phone rang loudly, disturbing my concentration. Oh bother, I thought to myself as the pages of the book flicked shut and I lost my place again.

I answered the phone to be greeted by the familiar voice of one of the Elders who informed me that a fellow witch was very ill and needed our help. All coven members were being called together to perform a very special healing ritual. The person concerned was a highly respected and much loved member of a neighbouring group and although elderly in years, had continued to practice Magic until very recently. Because of who the person was, there would be some very important guests from other covens coming to join us and it was made very clear this was going to be quite some gathering.

The date, time and venue had been carefully chosen by the Elders and preparations were already well under way. The ritual was set to take place between the next New Moon and Full Moon at a sacred site in North Cornwall. We had worked there before and knew the site well, the energies were pure and strong and I knew this would be an eventful gathering.

As soon as the telephone conversation was over I rang Claire and we arranged to meet the next day to make plans. Between us we managed to contact other members of our own coven and all necessary arrangements were made for us to join the ceremony in Cornwall.

It was a long journey, but we finally arrived at our hotel safe and sound with time to spare and having settled in quickly, we decided to take a walk along a nearby coastal path to help blow away the cobwebs. In no time at all the clear, clean Cornish air had worked its magic and we began to feel re-vitalised and ready for the task ahead.

The pathway was rugged and hard work, uphill and down, over stiles and through heavy wooden gates and after an hour or so, our legs began to ache and our faces had taken on a healthy, wind-swept, ruddy red glow.

"Crumbs", said Claire glancing in my direction, "we're looking more like the locals by the minute" and on that note we headed back toward the inviting warmth of the hotel and a nice hot cup of tea.

Our journey back was quiet as the mood between us changed from one of happy chatter to a more subdued and sombre atmosphere. We were beginning to prepare ourselves mentally for the task ahead later that evening.

The coven began to gather and the atmosphere was calm and hopeful. Everyone went about their business in an organised manner and there was an air of quiet respect as preparations began.

Once the initial Blessing of the Altar and casting of the Circle had taken place, I knew the real Magic was about to begin and the hairs on the back of my neck stood up at the mere thought of what might happen.

In rituals like this we make what is known as a 'Fith-Fath'. It is a representation of the subject of healing and can be a person or an animal, either way it is created with much love and great care.

During the ceremony, an incision was made down the centre of the Fith-Fath and various items such as a lock of the person's hair, a fingernail clipping, spittle and items from the five elements were placed inside it.

The High Priest then led the High Priestess to the Altar where she offered her hand and held it over the Fith-Fath. The High Priest withdrew his athame from its sheath and the hand of the High Priestess was cut with a small nick allowing one single drop of her blood to drip on to the Fith-Fath. Each member of the coven then approached the Altar and one by one leant over the working and gently and with intent, breathed a single breath into it.

As each Witch completed this part of the task they returned to the edge of the Circle and waited in silence. When the last person had breathed into the Fith-Fath, it was handed back to the High Priestess who then sealed it shut. She spoke the words of a healing spell over it and passed it around the Circle for each of us to do the same.

Claire and I waited patiently for it to reach our hands. Claire took it first and as she started to speak the words of her charm I noticed a strange look in her eyes. She glanced at me with an enquiring gaze, glanced back at the Fith-Fath, stuttered her words a little and then looked back at me. As she placed the Fith-Fath into my waiting hands she stared at me again and I noticed her hands were shaking slightly, but she said nothing. I held the subject gently, took a moment to compose myself and began to speak my words of spell and then it happened.

The Fith-Fath moved, I nearly dropped it. A small gasp left my lips, I looked at Claire who was already watching me intensely. She nodded a knowing nod and I knew she had felt it too, so this is what had startled her. This working was alive, no doubt about it and then as if in confirmation, the whole thing began to squirm in my hands again its movements clearly visible for all to see.

I could say nothing other than to carry on with my spell and pass it on around the Circle. I watched carefully as each person took hold of the Fith-Fath waiting to see if it moved again, but nothing happened and it remained still.

When the Fith-Fath had completed its tour of the Circle it was returned to rest upon the altar. One of the Elders began a chant and as we all joined in the whole Circle began to sway together in unison.

As the chanting grew louder energies around us rose from a gentle crescendo to an intensely powerful force making it difficult to stay on your feet and keep upright. The Circle was building an immense Cone of Power and everyone was being whipped into a powerful frenzy.

Suddenly, out of nowhere, appeared before us the most beautiful otherworldly electric blue light. It manifested right in the middle of the Circle rising sharply from the Earth. Just a tip at first, but as it rose higher and higher into the air its colour filled the entire space within the Circle. Even the Elders stood with their mouths open as we all stared at the spectacle before us and the Fith-Fath began to move again.

This time it rose slowly from the Altar and began to float toward the centre of the Circle. No one moved a muscle. It was as though it was being drawn into the heart of the cone like a vacuum and as it reached the centre of the cone it came to an abrupt halt and hung there suspended in mid-air.

There was a loud 'snap' as if the pages of a book had been slammed shut and the creature, for it surely was alive, and the blue light was gone.

# The Seashore Ritual

It was a beautiful summer's day in late August and after a long hot car journey a small group of friends and I arrived at the quaint old seaside town of Swanage in south Dorset.

We were greeted by a scene that would not have been out of place on a picture post card; shimmering blue sea, a beautiful sandy beach full of deck chairs and sandcastles, children playing gleefully on the sand and in the water, people paddling, people swimming and those who were just strolling along soaking up the sunshine and the ambience. The whole bay echoed to the sound of happy chatter and the call of ever hopeful seagulls just waiting to swoop mercilessly and snatch someone's ice cream.

We had been invited to join a local celebration honouring the seas and oceans of the world and arranged to meet at a popular watering hole down on the quayside.

Having finally found a car parking space we headed off to find the others, it wasn't a difficult task we just followed the sounds of raucous laughter and merriment.

On entering the pub garden, we found celebrations to be most well under way. There was music playing, people singing and dancing and generally having a whale of a time (no pun intended).

Most of the revellers were wearing costumes in shimmering shades of blue and jade to represent the colours of the sea. There were dolphins, turtles, mermaids, a seahorse, a fish, a crab and even a pirate. A lot of time and effort had gone into creating each one of the outfits and it was obvious how important this celebration was important to the local people. We were greeted warmly by all present and once our thirst had been quenched with an ice-cold drink, it was time to gather our belongings and play follow the leader.

The procession meandered its way lazily along the shoreline arousing much interest from everyone, particularly the holidaymakers. Clicking cameras went into overdrive as we passed by and I couldn't help wondering how they were going to explain this little lot amongst the holiday snaps.

The mood was jovial, spirits were high and the mile-long hike across the sands seemed to pass in a flash. Before we knew it, we had reached the north end of the beach and the place chosen for the ceremony.

Preparations began immediately and everyone was so immersed in what they were doing that no one had noticed a rather strange phenomenon taking place on the beach behind us.

When we first arrived at the shoreline people were still enjoying the late afternoon sunshine. Some were having a picnic, others were asleep in their deckchairs and children were busy fishing about in rock pools with their little plastic buckets and nets.

As people from our group gathered together ready for the ceremony to begin, an eerie silence had begun to descend. We looked around to find nearly everyone on the beach had disappeared and those remaining appeared to be beating a hasty retreat.

People were quite literally grabbing their belongings, tucking them under one arm, whilst practically dragging the children along the sand with the other. One or two people were running away from us, one shoe on and one shoe off and in all this haste, no one noticed the solitary canvas chair left abandoned on the sand.

The exodus was quite funny to watch and reminded me how such fear is born of ignorance. If only someone had bothered to ask us what we were doing I mused and as I looked up a tall, slim, bear chested young man came pounding across the sands heading toward us. He was wearing nothing, but a pair of cut-off jeans and a grin that stretched from ear to ear. His smile showed off a perfect set of brilliant white teeth, a feature against the tanned skin of his face and as he approached, he did exactly that, he asked us what we were doing.

His curiosity was welcomed whole heartedly and everyone took great delight in explaining what was going on. He seemed genuinely interested in what we were doing and when he asked to join our celebrations, he was accepted immediately. He explained he was with a small group of friends and asked if they might also be able to join us.

We agreed they could and with that, he sprinted off across the sand to the dunes behind, where apparently, they had been watching us for quite some time. He returned with three others and having warmly welcomed the newcomers, everyone settled and the ceremony finally began.

After the preliminary opening of the ceremony had taken place, outfits were removed and everyone entered the water. Some of us wore swimming costumes, others were happy to go into the sea fully clothed, either way it felt right to be in the sea. We waded through the water until we were about chest high in it then linked hands to form a Circle. As the last two people connected with each other a blast of pure energy coursed through each one of us like a bolt of lightning.

Something very special was about to happen and sure enough, it did.

It took a few moments to compose ourselves, but when everyone was ready a member of the group began to chant. One by one we all joined in until the voice of many, became the sound of one. The slow hypnotic melody continued for several minutes until, from above the sound came the voice of one man. He was asking us to remain very still and open our eyes. Following his instruction, the chanting dropped to a low crescendo before fading away to silence. We opened our eyes to be greeted by the sort of scene that only dreams are made of.

Behind us, not thirty feet away from the edge of the Circle, was a pod of dolphins playing in the sea.

Silently and gracefully they glided past us, first one way, then the other as though checking to make sure we were watching them. Satisfied they had our undivided attention, the show began. At first, just a few of the dolphins peeled away from the main pod dipping and diving into the rolling waves, disappearing and reappearing at will. Others joined the spectacle and began leaping in and out of the water like arching rainbows. The remainder of the pod showed of their gymnastic skills as they rolled over onto their back scooting across the surface of the sea using their tails to steer them. In these few glorious moments of sheer delight and playfulness they touched the hearts of us all.

We stood as still as statues, well as much as we could on moving sand. No one spoke, no one dared move a muscle, we were totally captivated watching the dolphins play. Then something else truly magical happened.

One of the dolphins broke away from the pod and swam straight toward us stopping just short from the edge of the Circle. He waited a while then began to nod his head, tapping his nose on the water as he did so. He repeated this movement several times stopping intermittently to look at us, then he did it all again.

Still no one moved. The dolphin began to come closer until eventually he was right behind the people at the edge of the Circle. Using the same nodding motion with his nose, he gently tapped one of them on the shoulder.

"Open the Circle", someone said and as the Circle opened, the dolphin swam right into its centre.

Slowly and gently, he rose out of the water to about half way up his body length, then slipped back down again and began to swim around the inner circle. He came to within inches away from each of us and the temptation was just too much as one by one, we held out our hands and he allowed us to touch him. His skin was warm and soft, his mouth gently curving up as if he were smiling.

Such a beautiful creature could not help, but radiate happiness and contentment.

He continued to circle round several times thoroughly enjoying all the attention when all of a sudden, he stopped right in front of me. I instinctively leant toward him and looking straight into his eyes I fell into the deepest pools of love I have ever known. In that instant I recognised and connected with an energy I had once been part of. I knew this mammal, not as a dolphin, as a man. I saw him as a man and I knew his soul. We stared into each other's eyes and without uttering a single word we spoke to each other.

It was one of the most amazing, ethereal experiences I have ever had and I cannot explain it any other way than it is written. Neither of us wanted to break the connection the bond was so strong, but when the time came I reluctantly let go and stepped back into Circle.

The dolphin turned and left the Circle heading back out to sea and his friends who were waiting for him. We watched the pod continue to play together, their silhouettes becoming smaller and smaller as further away they swam, until they reached the horizon and were gone.

By now the tide had turned and was on its way back in making it increasingly difficult to stand up. Reluctantly the ceremony was bought to a close and everyone headed back to dry land. It's hard work dragging a soaking wet, fully clothed body out of the water and as we reached the shore exhausted each one of us fell into a crumpled heap upon the sand. We sat in silence, soaking wet we may well have been, but we sat there staring out to sea, quite literally spellbound and with just one single question on our minds;

Did that truly just happen?

I looked over at our guests and saw they too were sat motionless, an unmistakable expression of total disbelief clearly written all over their faces. One of the young men kept staring at his hands first turning them one way, then the other. He just couldn't believe it, they were indeed the hands that had just touched a dolphin.

"Well, I don't know about anybody else", someone said breaking the silence, "but I most definitely need a drink. That was awesome, absolutely awesome…" and I watched as he carried on muttering to himself all the way along the beach.

"Wow, that was out of this world", said the young man who had first asked to join us. "Does that sort of thing happen all the time for you guys?"

The rest of us looked at each other.

"If only", someone joked and we all laughed.

The group made their way back to the pub on the quay and I could guess the topic of conversation for the rest of the evening.

*I stayed on the beach on my own for a while and remembered Atlantis.*

# The Hare

It was a beautiful sunny summer's afternoon and Claire and I were deep in the heart of the forest. We were busy foraging Nature's harvest ready to replenish our store of magical items. We had a basketful of twigs and barks, mushrooms, nuts, cones, berries and herbs, lichens, mosses, feathers and furs and all manner of strange things that to us, as Witches was indeed 'treasure'. On our return home, they would be carefully prepared and when ready each item would be lovingly stored and labelled ready for use.

We made a joke about how excited we were to be out 'Witchy shopping' as we called it fully aware that this was not quite the sort of thing that came to mind when most people use the term 'shopping'. Even so, we loved gathering our stores, there's always something very special about using items in magical spells that you have gathered and prepared yourself. They are special because they have absorbed some of your own energy and intention and are therefore, far more potent and powerful when used in magic.

We were both so engrossed in what we were doing that neither of us had noticed what was happening in the sky above us. The Sun had given way to some rather large big black clouds full to the brim with rain and about to burst right above us. Sure enough they did and we got drenched in about thirty seconds flat.

The rain heaved down, great big dollops of raindrops the size of peas and then came the hail and that was even bigger.

"Oops, do you think Mother Nature's telling us we've picked too much this afternoon?" I asked Claire.

"Well, if She wants it back", Claire replied, "she'll have to take it, cos I'm certainly not sticking this lot back on the trees and bushes. Oh dear, the car's miles away and it looks like this could be in for a while".

"Guess we'll just have to run for it then" I said.

We hurriedly gathered together all the goodies we'd collected and began our dash back to the car.

It was hard work trying to run in such heavy rain let alone hang on to the contents of our baskets without spilling everything. The rain was relentless slamming right into us making it difficult to see where we were going and that was just the problem, Claire didn't.

Next thing I knew there was an almighty thud, then a shriek and there was Claire, face down on the ground. She was completely immersed in the slippery, grey-brown mud and muck of the track and if it wasn't for the whites of her eyes as she looked up at me, no one would ever have known she was there.

"So, this is what a real live mud monster looks like", I said, trying very hard to stifle my giggles.

"Funny ha, ha", replied Claire.

"And don't even think about mentioning how good mud is for the skin 'coz right now, all I can think about is how many ponies have weed in it."

With that, I just had to let out the biggest peel of laughter, I couldn't hold on to it any longer. She did look a sight.

I bent down to help her up and as we struggled to free her from the mire she let out an almighty ear piercing shriek.

"Oh my goodness, how bad is it" I asked, almost too afraid to hear the answer.

"I'm alright I think", she said, "just caught my ankle awkwardly", but as she tried to get up there was another whelp of pain and we realised she had hurt herself quite badly.

It was obvious we were going to need help, but neither of us could get a signal on our phones so the only option left was to struggle on up the track.

Claire tried to hobble along best she could, but it wasn't long before we had to stop, she just couldn't do it. By now, the rain was torrential and we were slipping and sliding all over the place. I knew we needed help and I also knew I couldn't leave Claire alone. There was no other option, we would have to find shelter somewhere and sit it out.

Claire began to cry, her ankle was swelling badly, we were stuck in the middle of the forest, she was in pain and frightened.

"Chin up chicken", I said to her, "don't worry, we'll get you sorted, just need to get you out of this rain".

I've no idea where I got the strength from, but somehow, I managed to half drag, half carry her to the canopy of a giant yew tree.

I sat her down on a carpet of soft dry pine needles then found a pile of leaves covered in moss and used them to make a cushion to rest her leg on. Once I'd got her as comfortable as I could I headed off to pick some comfrey leaves and meadowsweet I had noticed growing nearby. These herbs contain ingredients that help draw out bruising and reduce inflammation and would be most useful in easing some of the pain in Claire's ankle.

We called out to each other all the time I was collecting the plants, it helped us both feel less vulnerable and before we knew it I was back at her side. Whilst Claire eased off her boot and sock I set to work crushing and tearing the herbs into tiny pieces. When I had enough to work with I wetted them in the rain then mashed and squeezed them together until they began to form a kind of paste. I applied the paste to Claire's ankle and secured it with her redundant sock.

"Now then", I said, sitting back to admire my handy work, "if we can get you to a better place of shelter I could try getting further up the track and see if I can summon help".

"Oh no, please don't leave me", replied Claire, "I just need to rest a while then I'm sure I'll be able to make it back to the car".

I doubted her optimism at this point, but could see in her eyes she did not want to be left alone. Not wishing to upset Claire any further, I decided to wait with her for the time being in the vain hope the storm would pass quickly. The afternoon was drawing to a close and the darkness of night would soon be upon us. With each passing minute, my concerns deepened, there was much marshland and far too many bogs in this part of the forest to be out here alone and lost at night.

We sat under the shelter of the yew tree both quiet and deep in thought, busy making our own silent plans I guess when out of the corner of my eye I saw a fern move. At first it was just the odd rustle then the movements became more and more obvious. Without a doubt, from deep within the undergrowth there was something, or someone, heading straight toward us.

"Did you see that?" asked Claire.

"I certainly did", came my reply and our gaze fixed upon the movement of the ferns as we waited for 'it' whatever 'it' was, to show itself. To our complete and utter amazement, right in front of us appeared the most magnificent, huge, brown, beautiful Hare.

As bold as brass he came right on up beside us and sat there staring at us as intently as we were staring at him. He turned to scamper off, hopped a few paces, turned back to see if we were watching him, went a bit further, then came back again. He repeated this pattern several times till in the end the penny dropped.

"I know this is going to sound completely off the wall", I said, "but I have the strangest feeling this hare wants us to follow him".

I turned to look at Claire, she was very pale and I could see the pain etched in her face, I knew I had to make a decision.

"Come on, lean on me", I continued, "I know this is totally nuts, but I think he's trying to help us. Let me take your weight and I promise we'll go real slow".

Claire didn't utter even the slightest resistance so I put one of her arms around my neck, tucked one of my arms around her waist and with a heave-ho, managed to get her to her feet. We began to follow the hare and after every few paces he would glance back to check we were still with him then off he'd go again. He was leading us way off the beaten track, the ground was rough and untrodden and most certainly not the easiest route to traverse, all things considered.

Ferns and brackens grabbed at our legs and tangled around our feet, we tripped and stumbled in deep rivets of mud and I felt sure it wouldn't be too much longer before we were both sporting sore ankles. Somehow, we managed to stay upright and continued to follow the hare.

"I hope there aren't any adders about", said Claire and I must admit the thought had crossed my mind. This was most definitely adder territory, but right now adders seemed the least of our problems. All I could think about was how exactly we were going to get out of here.

It wasn't long before we were in a dense part of the forest where the canopy of trees above was so thick they shielded us from the rain like an umbrella. The path we had been following suddenly took a sharp left turn and after only a few steps, the hare came to a prompt stop and sat himself down in a most meaningful manner. He turned his head slowly and purposefully to the right obviously wanting us to follow his gaze and as we did so, just a few paces away from the path, was an old wooden hut. The Hare had bought us to shelter.

Without hesitation, we approached the hut and pushed the door open. The wood of the door was dry and brittle and the bottom of it dragged along the floor noisily catching upon broken floor boards. We pushed it open far enough to squeeze inside and to our delight found a chair for Claire to sit on.

As old as the hut was, it was still full of equipment and after a good old rummage I found a hurricane lamp and a paraffin heater. Now all I needed was some paraffin and matches and we would have light and warmth.

"What do you think this hut is used for?" asked Claire, "I wonder who owns it?"

"I expect it's a twitchers' hideout or deer spotters den. It's certainly in the right place for that sort of thing", I replied whilst still hunting for fuel.

As our eyes adjusted to the darkness we discovered the walls of the hut were lined with wooden shelves packed tight to the rafters with books about the flora and fauna of the forest. In front of the window there was a small bench littered with a selection of artist's materials. There were sketch pads, palettes of dried up paint now cracked and turned to powder, brushes and pencils, jars and bottles strewn all over the place, their contents long since withered and perished.

I made my way over to the bench and as I did so I accidentally kicked something on the floor, a hollow 'tinny' sound rang out. I bent down to find out what it was and to my great delight found a fuel can, paraffin if I wasn't mistaken from the odour. The can was almost empty, but there did appear to be a small amount of liquid left sloshing around in the bottom. It wasn't much, but it would be enough to give us a little heat and light for now, if only I could find some matches, and there they were.

Tucked into the corner of a broken window frame was a bright yellow box of Swan vesta matches. I shook the box tentatively and a smile spread across my face at the unmistakable sound of rattling matches. 'Thank you Goddess' I said to myself.

I carefully poured a little of the liquid into the bottom of the hurricane lamp and the remainder into the stove tray. As the fuel gave up its familiar odour I was momentarily transported back to my childhood.

Precious memories of time spent watching my Dad as he went around the house each morning lighting the paraffin heaters in the lounge and the bathroom. He did this every day before he went to work so that the two rooms would be warm and cosy for when me and my brothers were getting ready for school. Little did I know what a valuable lesson those mornings were teaching me.

"Ah well, here goes", I said to Claire, as I struck a match on the side of the box. "Fingers crossed".

"And everything else", came her reply.

The match lit first strike and as each wick caught I noticed how the flame first burned a deep orange colour then changed to an almost cobalt blue. We had light and heat and all was well for now.

Having got things sorted in the hut I decided to look outside for the hare, perhaps he might be coaxed inside to share the shelter with us. He was nowhere to be seen and I couldn't help feeling disappointed. I felt guilty for not having thanked him for his help and guidance and that made me sad.

It was thundering and lightning by now so I closed the door resigned to the fact we would be there for the duration of the storm. To help distract Claire from the pain in her ankle I suggested we look at the sketches and paintings in the books on the bench.

Even though they were faded we could still see how intricate and beautiful they were. Whoever the artist was it was obvious they possessed a deep love and understanding of Nature.

We quickly became totally engrossed, captivated even, by the incredible collection of artwork and for a short while we were totally lost in the paintings.

That was, until a broom that had been resting against the wall on the other side of the hut, flew across the room and fell on the floor at our feet. OK, so what exactly are we supposed to do with this? I asked myself and the penny dropped.

Reaching forward, I motioned for Claire to grab my arm and as she did so I pulled her up onto her feet and wedged the broom under her arm. It fitted like a glove, we had ourselves a crutch.

The storm passed and the darkness of the forest was pierced by rays of brilliant sunshine. It was time to make our move.

I turned off the lamp and heater, thanked the hut for its shelter and hospitality and closed the door behind us as we left. We had no idea in which direction to travel so it seemed like the most logical thing to do was go back the way we came.

"You know in magic tricks the rabbit usually disappears then re-appears, well if Hare's can do the same trick, now would be a good time to make an appearance don't you think?" asked Claire hopefully.

"It would appear they can", I replied, pointing toward a clump of gorse bushes alight with their tiny yellow flowers. There he was as big and bold as ever, busily preening himself after the soaking he'd got from the rain.

He shot us a glare as though we had disturbed his personal grooming session, then shook himself off and proceeded to lead the way in his usual manner; a few hops forward and a glance back to check we were following him.

Having a make shift crutch to help Claire along this time made it so much easier to keep up with our new-found friend and to our great relief, it wasn't long before we arrived back at the car. I bundled Claire into the back seat so she could sit with her foot raised to ease the swelling and once she was settled I turned to thank the Hare. He was nowhere to be seen, he had vanished into thin air, once again!

"Well there's a surprise", I said to Claire, "looks like rabbits and Hare's do go to the same school of performing arts. Now I've got a question for you. How did he know we were trying to get back to the car and how on earth did he know where it was?"

"I was going to ask you those exact same questions", replied Claire.

I called out our grateful thanks in the hope he would hear them anyway, started the engine and set off homeward bound.

Claire made a good recovery and a few weeks later we decided it was time to return the broom to the hut.

It was a beautiful sunny afternoon not a cloud in the sky and our journey to the forest was a pleasure. We parked the car in the same place as before and headed off up the beaten track. Our plan was to find the yew tree we had first sheltered under then follow the smaller path through the bracken to the hut.

We found the yew tree quickly, but no way could we find the path through the bracken. In fact, we couldn't find another pathway anywhere at all. The vegetation was dense and unyielding and it was obvious no one and nothing had made its way through this lot for a very long time.

"Perhaps this isn't the same tree or the same place after all", said Claire.

I was just about to suggest we start looking elsewhere when I spotted a pile of rotting herbs in a heap at the base of the tree. I called Claire over.

"See this", I said, "they're the remains of the herbs I used to make the poultice for your ankle. We're in the right place alright, we just can't find the path".

"Maybe there isn't one", she replied in a rather 'matter of fact' tone and I couldn't help smiling at the irony of acceptance over such a strange occurrence. After all, we both knew there was a path here somewhere. We had walked it with the Hare just a few weeks before.

"Oh well, guess that's it then", I said, "don't know about you, but I really don't fancy trying to beat my way through this lot. Let's call it a day, at least we tried".

We knew the hut couldn't be too far from the yew tree so chances were at some time or another the owner of the hut might just pass this way. That being the case, if we left the broom propped up against the tree they might spot it on their way past and be able to return it to the hut.

Having wedged the broom securely up against the tree we were just about to leave when the most beautiful springer spaniel came bounding up to us panting loudly, tail wagging furiously. The spaniel was closely followed by a man sporting a brace of pheasants slung over one shoulder and a half – cocked gun folded over the other.

"Down Bess", he called to his dog, "gently now".

He stopped and looked at us with a rather, almost comical blank expression on his face.

"Don't often see folk this far into the woods", he barked, "especially you being women an' all".

Very observant of him I thought, rather sarcastically.

"We were looking for the little wooden hut that's not far from here I ventured in reply, but we can't seem to find the track that leads to it".

For a moment or two the man said nothing, he just stood there staring at us, his face a mask for an enquiring mind. He was obviously weighing us up before making any response so we waited in silence.

"And why might you be looking for the hut then, if I might ask?" he said, rather protectively.

Throwing caution to the wind we explained the series of events that had taken place leading up to our borrowing the broom and coming back here to return it. As we told our story the man listened intently and I noticed how his stance appeared to soften as our tale unfolded.

When we had finished talking he made his way over to a fallen tree trunk nearby where he sat himself down and proceeded to tell us the following: "Many Moons ago, there was indeed a hut deep in the forest. It was the home of an artist, a man who spent his life living and working with Nature.

He was well known by the local people and not just for his paintings. He was a wonderful healer by all accounts and people came to him for charms and potions and all sorts of things. Some said he was a Witch, but I don't think anyone asked him about that. We knew what we knew and that was that, never really needed to ask anymore. Suffice to say, he was a nice man, well- liked by everyone who met him and that's all that really matters. And then he was gone. No one knew where he had come from and no one knew where he went too. He vanished as mysteriously as he arrived".

The man continued.

"As for his hut, well, the locals decided it must remain exactly as he left it just in case one day he might return. So far, he never has, not in human form anyway. Some believe he came from the forest itself and that's where he has returned".

The man finished talking and began to push himself up from the tree trunk as if making his move to leave.

"Excuse me, I said, could you explain what you mean by *'the man returned to the forest'?"*

"Of course,", he replied, "folk round 'ere believe he never left the forest, he's still roaming the area, but not as a man, oh no, he is often seen around here as a Hare".

The End

Made in the USA
Lexington, KY
21 December 2017